D0454649

AL QAEDA

AL QAEDA

Brotherhood of Terror

Paul L. Williams

ALPHA
A Pearson Education Company

PROPERTY OF
NEWBERG HIGH SCHOOL
LIBRARY

Copyright © 2002 by Paul L. Williams

All rights reserved. No part of this book shall be reproduced, stored in a retrieval system, or transmitted by any means, electronic, mechanical, photocopying, recording, or otherwise, without written permission from the publisher. No patent liability is assumed with respect to the use of the information contained herein. Although every precaution has been taken in the preparation of this book, the publisher and author assume no responsibility for errors or omissions. Neither is any liability assumed for damages resulting from the use of information contained herein.

International Standard Book Number: 0-02-864352-6
Library of Congress Catalog Card Number: 2001099421

03 02   8 7 6 5 4 3 2 1

Interpretation of the printing code: The rightmost number of the first series of numbers is the year of the book's printing; the rightmost number of the second series of numbers is the number of the book's printing. For example, a printing code of 02-1 shows that the first printing occurred in 2002.

Printed in the United States of America

Note: This publication contains the opinions and ideas of its author. It is intended to provide helpful and informative material on the subject matter covered. It is sold with the understanding that the author and publisher are not engaged in rendering professional services in the book. If the reader requires personal assistance or advice, a competent professional should be consulted.

The author and publisher specifically disclaim any responsibility for any liability, loss, or risk, personal or otherwise, which is incurred as a consequence, directly or indirectly, of the use and application of any of the contents of this book.

Trademarks: All terms mentioned in this book that are known to be or are suspected of being trademarks or service marks have been appropriately capitalized. Alpha Books and Pearson Education, Inc., cannot attest to the accuracy of this information. Use of a term in this book should not be regarded as affecting the validity of any trademark or service mark.

B 26147

Contents

Introduction

In his *Summa Theologica,* St. Thomas Aquinas taught us that all clear thinking comes from making distinctions. But in the present war on terrorism, distinctions have become muddled, making clear thinking all but impossible. One terrorist group transmogrifies into another terrorist group. The State Department's Comprehensive List of Terrorists released on November 29, 2001, included 153 groups, entities, and individuals whose assets have been blocked by Executive Order. Some of them are known to have engaged in terrorist acts under the Al Qaeda umbrella. Others are suspected of having done so, and still others are thought to have some form of association with what could be described as a global Islamic extremist consortium.

As we approached the end of 2001, investigators had yet to learn how Al Qaeda was organized beyond what was known of its leadership structure and the existence of worldwide cells. The end of the battle in Afghanistan inevitably prompted rampant speculation as to who would be next: the Abu Sayyaf in the Philippines, the al-Jihad in Egypt, the Hizballah in Lebanon, the Armed Islamic Group (GIA) in Algeria, the Islamic Movement of Uzbekistan, or the Group Roubaix of Canada. But as soon as these groups are eliminated, others will probably arise to carry on *jihad* (struggle) against the United States, Israel, and Muslim regimes that have abandoned the values of pure Islam. They may include the Asbat al-Ansar in Lebanon, the Harakat ul-Ansar and the Hezb ul-Mujahideen in Pakistan, the Islamic Group in Egypt, the Lebanese Partisans League, and the Libyan Islamic

Fighting Group. And when these groups are vanquished, still others will emerge: the Salafist Group for Call and Combat (GSPD) in Algeria, the Jamiat Ulema-e-Islam (JUI) in Pakistan, the Bayt al-Imam in Jordan, the al-Jihad in Bangladesh, and the Partisans Movement in Kashmir. And behind these lurk more and more groups—in all corners of the world, even in Oklahoma and Utah.

Some of these organizations are amorphous. They are not linked to any national group but are pan-Islamic in scope and appeal: the Islamic Advice and Reform Committee, the Islamic Jihad, the Talaa al Fath (Vanguards of Conquest), and Hamas. There are distinctions among them based on differences in their history and their political circumstances, but they are alike in their fanaticism, and they threaten a common enemy—the United States.

The enemy now facing the United States and its allies cannot be defeated by normal tactics and techniques. It represents a hydra: When one head is severed, another immediately appears. Similarly, there is no national enemy in this war as in other wars. If, as President Bush said in his address to a Joint Session of Congress on September 20, 2001 ...

> "Our war on terror begins with Al Qaeda, but it does not
> end there. It will not end until every terrorist group of
> global reach has been found, stopped, and defeated."

There will be invasions of Lebanon, Iraq, the Philippines, Sudan, Egypt, Pakistan, Algeria, Yemen, Lebanon, Somalia, Kenya, and so on. That—and much more in the way of security, freezing of financial assets, intelligence, and counterterrorism—is what it would take to eradicate every viper's nest, every manifestation of Islamic extremism, every cry of jihad in the world. It is an impossible task that, perhaps, can only end in futility.

"How do you stop a mullah in a mosque in Kabul from preaching jihad?" a senior British intelligence officer involved in the global investigations of Al Qaeda recently asked. "We're not a global Gestapo. How can we stop them?"

Other distinctions are also becoming muddled in the present war on terrorism, including the distinction between economics, politics, and theology.

The war is economic. It is caused by the desire of the Middle East to control their own natural resources, including natural gas and oil, without foreign (that is, U.S.) involvement.

The war is political. It is caused by U.S. support of Israel and the proliferation of American military bases in Muslim nations.

The war is religious. Bin Laden and his followers are holy warriors who are conducting a struggle against infidels in keeping with their interpretation of the teachings of the Prophet Muhammad.

The U.S. government has been unequivocal in its position that this is a war on terrorism, not a war against Islam. Indeed the idea of a global religious war at the dawn of the twenty-first century seems preposterous. Such wars, we believed, ended with the Crusades. But for Al Qaeda and other extremist groups, historic distinctions, distinctions of time and place, don't seem to exist. This is evident in many of Osama bin Laden's statements, including this passage from his 1996 "Declaration of War Against the Americans Occupying the Land of the Two Holy Mosques":

> "Our Lord, the people of the cross had come with their horses and occupied the land of the two Holy Places.

And the Zionist Jews fiddling as they wish with the Al
Aqsa Mosque, the route of the ascendance of the messenger of Allah (Allah's blessings and salutations on him).
Our Lord, shatter their gathering, divide them among
themselves, shake the earth under their feet and give us
control of them. Our Lord, we take refuge in you from
their deeds and take us as a shield between us and
them."

There is another distinction that is being obliterated. Although
many of the issues that Al Qaeda speaks to resonate in the Islamic
world, most Muslims are opposed to, even repelled by, its terrorist acts. Continuous and persistent military action by the United
States against Al Qaeda and its hundreds of tentacles—action
that is mandated by September 11, 2001—can only result in a
bifurcation of the Islamic and the Judeo-Christian worlds. Such
a bifurcation can bring about nothing but increased hostility in
the coming years.

The lines are dissolving, and the circles are becoming con-
centric.

My involvement with Al Qaeda came about when I was
obtaining information for the FBI regarding members of the
Russian Mafia from Little Odessa in New York and a stolen car
ring in northeastern Pennsylvania. The Russians were involved in
more than stolen cars. They heisted a new and expensive BMW
or Mercedes, bought a wreck of the same model from a junkyard,
switched serial numbers from the wreck to the stolen car,
repainted the car, and transferred the title across state lines. It was
a neat and very lucrative scheme. The Russians were also
involved in selling vast quantities of heroin along the entire east
coast in conjunction with their Sicilian counterparts. The drugs
flowed into the United States from the harbor of Gdansk,

Poland. They came to Poland from Turkey. The opium merchants of Turkey obtained their product from the poppy fields of Afghanistan. The poppy fields and warehouses of Afghanistan were controlled by members of Al Qaeda. Indeed, Al Qaeda possessed the laboratory technology and sophisticated facilities to refine the crop into choice Number Four heroin. But the trail didn't end in Afghanistan. It led to a warehouse in Chechnya, where former KGB members sold "nuclear suitcases" and other weapons of mass destruction to representatives of Osama bin Laden.

Few investigations were more intricate and circuitous. One nefarious activity dissolved into another, with a trail leading from a sleepy city in Pennsylvania to the poppy fields of Afghanistan to a weapons market in Chechnya.

Many of the KGB officials who conducted these sales are now living the good life in the United States. Several have settled in Coney Island, where they make millions stealing and selling high-priced cars to rich young Americans.

Chronology

1988	Al Qaeda's birthyear. It is founded by Osama bin Laden, Muhammed Atef, and Ayman al-Zawahiri to continue the jihad internationally. "The Base" is headquartered in Afghanistan and Peshawar, Pakistan.
November 24, 1989	A remote-control bomb kills Abdallah Azzam and two of his sons in Peshawar.
1989	Bin Laden returns to Saudi Arabia to work in his family's construction company. He protests the presence of U.S. military bases in his homeland and begins importing arms from Yemen allegedly to mount a rebellion against King Faud.
1990–1991	Iraq invades Kuwait, and the United States forms an international coalition to oppose the invasion.
September 1, 1991	Saudi government expels bin Laden from the kingdom.
September 15, 1991	Bin Laden buys a comfortable brick-and-stucco house in Sudan and another house for family retreats on the Blue Nile.
1992	Civil war erupts in Afghanistan. Al Qaeda announces that U.S. military forces in Saudi Arabia, Yemen, and the Horn of Africa should be attacked.

September 1992   Ramzi Yousef leaves an Al Qaeda "guest-house" in Peshawar and travels to New York to plan the bombing of the World Trade Center. Yousef meets with Sheikh Omar Abd al Rahman in Manhattan.

December 29, 1992   Al Qaeda's first terrorist hit. A bomb is detonated at a hotel in Yemen, killing one tourist. The bomb was intended to kill U.S. troops who had been deployed to Somalia on a humanitarian mission.

February 23, 1993   A car bomb explodes in the World Trade Center in New York, killing six and wounding more than a thousand people.

October 3, 1993   Osama bin Laden later claims responsibility for training the Somali tribesmen who assaulted U.S. troops in Mogadishu, Somalia, killing 18 and injuring scores more.

1994–1995   Al Qaeda is linked to a series of plans that are not carried out: the assassination of Pope John Paul II in Manila, simultaneous bombings of the U.S. and Israeli embassies in Manila and other Asian capitals, and the assassination of President Clinton during his visit to the Philippines. The group also initiates a series of pogroms on Christians in the Sudan.

July 11, 1994   With funding from bin Laden, Khaled Al Fauwaz opens the Advice and Reformation Committee in London.

December 1994   Terry Nichols meets with Ramzi Yousef in Manila to plot the bombing of the Alfred P. Murrah Federal Building in Oklahoma City.

February 7, 1995	Ramzi Yousef, the mastermind behind the World Trade Center bombing, is arrested in Pakistan and extradited to the United States.
April 19, 1995	The Oklahoma City bombing.
June 26, 1995	A botched attempt to assassinate Egyptian President Hosni Mubarak in Ethiopia is claimed by Egypt's Al-Gama'a al-Islamiyya, some of whose leaders escape to Afghanistan to become allied with Al Qaeda.
October 1995	Sheikh Omar Abd al-Rahman and nine others are convicted of conducting a terrorist conspiracy against the United States. The blind Sheikh is the spiritual leader of two Egyptian extremist groups associated with Al Qaeda.
November 13, 1995	A truck bomb explodes outside Saudi Arabia's National Guard Communications Center in Riyadh, killing two Indians and five U.S. servicemen.
Spring 1996	Bin Laden is forced to leave Sudan and accepts the new Taliban government's offer of safe haven in Afghanistan.
June 25, 1996	A massive truck bomb explodes outside Khobar Towers in Dhahran, Saudi Arabia, killing 19 American soldiers and injuring scores more.
August 23, 1996	Bin Laden issues his "Declaration of War Against the Americans Occupying the Land of the Two Holy Mosques" from the Hindu Kush Mountains in Afghanistan. He calls upon all Muslims to join the jihad.

November 10, 1997 Al Qaeda members gun down four American oil workers in Pakistan.

November 13, 1997 Ramzi Yousef and Eyad Ismail are convicted of conspiracy in the World Trade Center bombing. Both are sentenced to 240 years in prison.

February 23, 1998 Al Qaeda officials, along with the Egyptian Jihad Group, Al-Jihad, the Jihad Movement of Bangladesh, and the Pakistan Scholars Society, endorse a *fatwa* (edict) under the heading "International Islamic Front for Jihad on the Jews and Crusaders." The fatwa instructs Muslims to kill Americans, including civilians, wherever they can be found.

August 7, 1998 Two truck bombs explode moments apart outside the U.S. embassies in Kenya and Tanzania, killing 301 people, including 12 Americans, and wounding more than 5,000 others.

August 20, 1998 In retaliation for the embassy bombings, the United States launches cruise missile attacks on several terrorist camps in Afghanistan and on a pharmaceutical plant in Sudan that is thought to be linked to bin Laden.

September 18, 1998 U.S. intelligence thwarts the bombing of the U.S. Embassy in Kampala, Uganda, by Al Qaeda operatives.

September 23, 1998 British authorities arrest seven suspected Al Qaeda members in London.

November 4, 1998 U.S. Attorney General Janet Reno indicts Osama bin Laden and Muhammed Atef, Al Qaeda's military commander, on a total of 301 counts of murder in connection with the U.S. Embassy bombings in East Africa.

July 7, 1999 President Clinton imposes sanctions against the Taliban for harboring bin Laden, who is using Ariana (Afghanistan's national airline) for terrorist and drug-smuggling operations. The sanctions prohibit U.S. trade and transactions with the Taliban and freeze all Taliban assets in the United States.

October 16, 1999 The UN Security Council imposes sanctions on the Taliban until bin Laden is expelled from the country. The sanctions prohibit all commerce between member states and the Afghan government.

December 1999 The FBI obtains from Jordan copies of a six-volume manual used by bin Laden to train Al Qaeda recruits. The manual had been in the possession of terrorists who were arrested in Jordan while planning New Year's attacks in Israel.

December 14, 1999 Ahmed Ressam is arrested in Port Angeles, Washington, for possession of 110 pounds of urea, 14 pounds of sulfate, and 4 homemade timers. Ressam had been planning to blow up Los Angeles International Airport when the clock struck midnight on January 1, 2000.

December 15, 1999   Jordanian officials arrest 13 terrorists for planning to blow up the Radisson Hotel in Amman, Jordan.

February 22, 2000   Bin Laden is reported to be in failing health, with plans to turn over control of Al Qaeda to Ayman al-Zawahiri.

March 10, 2000   President Clinton's planned visit to a village in Bangladesh is called off because of a terrorist threat linked to Al Qaeda.

March 17, 2000   News reports state that bin Laden is dying of kidney failure. Bin Laden later says he was amused by the conjecture.

October 5, 2000   The USS *Cole* is attacked in a suicide bombing that kills 17 and wounds 39 American sailors in Aden Harbor, Yemen.

October 31, 2000   The Jamiat Ulema-e-Islam warns that it will retaliate against the United States if it attacks Afghanistan or bin Laden.

November 1, 2000   Mamdouh Mahmud Salim, charged with conspiracy in the East African Embassy attacks, stabs one prison guard in the eye and another in the stomach and sprays others with irritants during a failed escape from the Metropolitan Correctional Center in New York.

December 19, 2000   The UN Security Council passes Resolution 1333, banning all military aid to the Taliban in an effort to shut down Al Qaeda terrorist camps in Afghanistan.

December 28, 2000 German police arrest four members of Al
Qaeda in Frankfurt, Germany, and uncover
a large amount of weapons and explosives.
Of the four arrested, one is an Algerian,
one a French national, and two are Iraqis.

February 6, 2001 Jamal al-Fadl, known only as CS-1 prior to
taking the stand, testifies at the Southern
District Court of New York and provides a
detailed account of the inner workings of
Al Qaeda.

February 18, 2001 President Ali Abdullah Saleh of Yemen
announces the arrest of two Al Qaeda
terrorists in connection with the October
2000 attack on the USS *Cole.*

February 26, 2001 At a wedding reception for his son, bin
Laden recites one of his poems. The ode
celebrates the *Cole* bombing and the killing
of American Naval personnel.

July 1, 2001 Djamel Begal, an Algerian member of Al
Qaeda, is arrested in the United Arab
Emirates upon the discovery of his plot to
crash a helicopter into the U.S. Embassy in
Paris.

September 11, 2001 Nineteen terrorists hijack four U.S. airliners, which they crash into the twin towers
of the World Trade Center in New York;
the Pentagon in Arlington, Virginia; and a
field in Shanksville, Pennsylvania. Authorities believe that the fourth plane's intended
target was the U.S. Capitol or the White
House.

Based on Alexander and Swetnam's Usama bin Laden's al-Qaida: Profile of a Terrorist Network
(Transnational Publishers, Inc., 2001).

Prologue

Meeting Al Qaeda and Staying Alive

> "There is a simple way to stay alive among the terrorists.
> No ceremony is involved in becoming a Muslim. All
> you need to do is say, 'There is no god but Allah, and
> Muhammad is his prophet.'"
>
> —"Tex Barker," soldier-for-hire

At the annual Soldiers of Fortune convention in Las Vegas, you can obtain things that are not available anywhere else. If you make the right connection, you can purchase an unregistered Saturday night special—a .38 Harrington and Richardson—for $300. On the upscale side, by mentioning the right name to a vendor, you can obtain the Uzi or AK-47 of your dreams for less than $5,000.

If you are a representative of a rebel force in a banana republic you can secure the services of a mercenary or a team of mercenaries. Many of the soldiers-for-hire are former Green Berets, SEALs, or Rangers. They meander through the crowd in army fatigues, with shaved heads and drooping mustaches. They've served in such places as El Salvador, Nicaragua, Myanmar, Bosnia, and Albania. They think of themselves not as shooters, but trainers. They introduce themselves not as paid assassins, but as repairmen. One such repairman at the 2001 Convention is Tex Barker (not his real name). He is 55 years old and has a withered face, steel-gray eyes, and a body without an ounce of fat.

Barker recently returned from a trip to Kabul, Afghanistan, for a military organization in Pretoria, South Africa. His objective was to purchase weapons from the stockpiles of Osama bin Laden's terrorist group, Al Qaeda, and from the gun factories in Darra Adam Khel in Pakistan. For his efforts, he received $2,000 a day plus expenses. The pay wasn't enough, he says. Kabul is one place he never wants to see again:

> "The members of Al Qaeda are fanatics. They are not cold-blooded killers. These guys think they will please God by blowing your brains out. You can't reason with them. You can't talk to them. Hell, you can't even look at them."

In Kabul, because Barker's purpose was to conduct clandestine meetings with Al Qaeda, he could not stay at the UN mansion (equipped with an exercise room, satellite television, and a bar) that was an oasis for journalists and ambassadors. He stayed at the Inter-Continental Hotel at a rate of $100 a night. He said he was lucky to get a room, because the city was crowded with refugees. At the hotel, he was shown to a room reserved for Christians and Jews and told not to leave without permission and not to socialize with the other guests. The room was stripped of all amenities, and the electricity, 20v/50 Hz, flowed only intermittently. The same was true of the tap water.

Barker spent much of his time watching the traffic from a window. The shops opened at 8 A.M. and closed before noon. The streets were crowded with minibuses, cabs, and pack animals—horses, donkeys, and camels. A camel, he later discovered, could be rented for $10 (U.S.) a day, and a guide could be had for $20 plus *baksheesh* (tip). But Barker was here, not to see the sights, but to conduct business.

Representatives of Al Qaeda always met him in his hotel room, never in the lobby. In fact, he was warned never to venture into the lobby because, in the jihad, all Europeans (Christian and Jewish) are targets.

The few times Barker left his room he was obliged to wear a yellow ribbon on his arm to identify him as a non-Muslim. A yellow ribbon also was tied to the door of his room. According to a fatwa (edict), there was to be no association between the people of the House of Islam and the people of the House of War (everyone else).

The negotiations over weapons were his only source of amusement. There was neither a television nor a radio in his room. The city offered no movie theaters. There were no liquor stores, let alone a bar or a nightclub. Worse, there were no women. Women were forbidden to appear in public without a male family member. And even when women did go out in public, they were obliged to appear in full *burqa* from head to toe, so that no part of their body was visible.

One day, as Barker was looking out the window, a member of Al Qaeda warned him not to stare at the covered and veiled women, because any sign of lust was punishable by death.

There was no possibility of sightseeing. Even if he had been permitted to leave the hotel, Barker would have found that the Kabul Museum, which had once possessed one of the finest collections of antiquities in Asia, had been looted of its prized possessions. And he couldn't have meandered around the crumbling walls of the ancient citadel, Bala Hissar, or the fabled Gardens of Babur without the risk of stepping on a land mine.

Barker concluded his business, without ever meeting bin Laden, and was then obliged to wait for the transfer of funds. When this was accomplished to the satisfaction of the terrorists, he was taken by taxi from Kabul to the airport at Dubai. The taxi cost $175, plus the customary baksheesh. For protection against brigands, Barker was advised to secure the services of an Al Qaeda guard.

When I queried him about how he managed to get out of Afghanistan alive after Al Qaeda had received his payments, Barker said that he'd known what to do and what not to do from other "repairmen" or "trainers" who had conducted business with bin Laden and the terrorists:

- Do not make sexual remarks about women or tell an off-color joke. Maintain a sober and serious manner. Speak only when necessary.

- Make no mention of religion. Above all, do not smile or sound flippant when mentioning the Koran or the name of the Prophet.

- Do not wear anything that has religious significance, such as a cross or the Star of David.

- Do not squeeze hands when shaking them. It is a sign of aggression. After shaking hands, touch your chest as a gesture of submission and respect.

- Never touch a member of Al Qaeda or any other Islamic terrorist group with your left hand. The Muslims wash their privates and wipe their backsides with this hand. It is deemed unclean.

- Never pass food with your left hand.

- Never stand to urinate in the presence of the terrorists. This is a sign of disrespect. They always sit or squat to empty their bladders.

- Never blow your nose in the presence of a member of Al Qaeda. This is a grievous insult.

- Never eat while walking around—not even a candy bar. It is a sign of inhospitality and disrespect.

- Never take pictures without permission. Above all, never take photos of women, the infirm, or the elderly.

- Never gaze at a woman, not even in passing. When a woman, even in full burqa, appears before you, cast your eyes to the ground.

- Never gaze at a man, not even in passing. A member of Al Qaeda might assume you are gay, and all gays are an abomination before Allah.

- Never express admiration for any object belonging to a terrorist. This will compel him to give it to you as a gesture of hospitality. He will then only be able to reclaim the object through your sudden demise.

- Never drink alcoholic beverages in any Islamic country. This shows disrespect for the teaching of the Prophet.

- Never point the soles of your feet at a host. It represents an implied threat.

- Never wear your shoes in a Muslim shrine or mosque. If you are invited to the house of a terrorist, remove your shoes at the front door.

- Never carry religious tracts or objects of religious devotion (such as a rosary or a prayer book). It will imply that you intend to proselytize the Christian or Jewish religion.

- Never violate the Holy Day of Friday by loud and impious behavior.

- Never read a book with a lurid title or a magazine with lewd content.

Barker says there are many other tips for staying alive in the company of members of Al Qaeda and other terrorist groups. But in the final analysis, they may be of little value. The jihad is against all unbelievers; if they do not submit to the will of Allah, they must be put to death without mercy.

There is one simple way to stay alive among the terrorists. No ceremony is involved in becoming a Muslim. All you need to do is say, "There is no god but Allah, and Muhammad is his prophet." Once you proclaim these two tenets of Islamic faith, you are not required to produce further proof of your faith and conviction. From that point on, you are accepted into the Muslim brotherhood and granted all the rights of any believer under Islamic law. This means that neither bin Laden nor any member of his organization can spill your blood and remain a pious Muslim. But it also means that you must participate in the jihad.

Once you've become a Muslim, there are a few other hitches. In addition to flashing a smile and the peace sign when you meet with the members of Al Qaeda, you should be able to recite several *surahs*, or passages from the Koran. This will convince the terrorists that you are not kidding about your conversion.

Moreover, when the name or title of the Prophet is mentioned, you must cry out the invocation *"salla-Liahu alaihi wasalam"* ("May God bless him and give him peace"), or the equally valid, *alaihi-s-salam* ("Peace be with him").

If you are male, you will have to expose your member to show proof that you have been circumcised.

The ways of Barker and his mechanics are not those of mainstream Westerners any more than the ways of the Taliban are those of mainstream Muslims. That was apparent when the Northern Alliance liberated Kabul on November 14, 2001. The residents of Kabul celebrated the departure of the fundamentalists with loud music and dancing in the streets. Men waited in line at barber shops for a close shave, and there were radio and television broadcasts again. All seemed to return to normal, except for the fact that women remained sequestered, unsure of what the new rules might be. The majority of Afghans, despite their beards and burqas, were not really religious extremists. They were simply practicing the art of staying alive.

1

Inside Al Qaeda

"The brothers who conducted the operation, all they knew was that they had a martyrdom operation and we asked each of them to go to America, but they didn't know anything about the operation, not even one letter. But they were trained and we did not reveal the operation to them until they were there and just before they boarded the planes."

—Osama bin Laden, from amateur video recorded in Kandahar, Afghanistan (circa November 9, 2001), released by the Pentagon, December 13, 2001

Until recently, Jamal Ahmed al-Fadl was known throughout the CIA only as CS-1, "Confidential Source One." The information provided by al-Fadl and by Ali Abul Nazzar has been verified by other Al Qaeda defectors and by information left on computer disks in Nairobi, Kenya.

In February 2001 al-Fadl became a key witness in the trial of four Al Qaeda members for the August 1998 suicide bombings of the U.S. embassies in Kenya and Tanzania that killed 301 people.

With the financial support of the Farouq Mosque in New York, al-Fadl had set off in 1988 for Peshawar, the dusty and miserable Pakistani border town that was home to hundreds of thousands of Afghan refugees and a training center for new recruits in Al Qaeda's holy war.

At the training camp, al-Fadl learned to fire a Russian-made Kalashnikov rifle, to pick planes out of the sky with United States–supplied Stingers and other surface-to-air rockets, and to pack plastic explosives in a Samsonite suitcase. He also met Ali Abul Nazzar, who hailed from Newark, New Jersey.

After several weeks the young recruit from Brooklyn was summoned before the new emir (chief), Osama bin Laden, who resided in Peshawar's cramped guesthouse chambers and gardens. Al-Fadl became a close associate of the ascetic Saudi exile and traveled with him to an explosives training camp in the battle-scarred town of Khost. Khost was where bin Laden had formed Al Qaeda.

All members of the organization were asked to sign agreements that they would devote their lives to the submission of all creation to the will of Allah. Al-Fadl signed the document as one of Al Qaeda's founding members. Then he took the *bayat* (oath of allegiance) to Osama bin Laden, which involved fasting, self-castigation with a whip made of small chains, and days of indoctrination.

(Courtesy FBI)

Osama bin Laden.

Al Qaeda's Structure

Al-Fadl explains how Al Qaeda is structured (as of early 2001):

At the head is the emir, Osama bin Laden.

Beneath bin Laden is the Shura Council that consists of a group of mullahs (those who are learned in religious law) and religious leaders who chart the jihad. The leading lieutenants of the group were identified by al-Fadl and others as follows:

- **Muhammed Atef,** a.k.a. Abu Hafs el Masry, Abdul Aziz Abu Sitta, Abu Hafs Taysir, Sheik Taysir Abdullah, Abu Fatima, Taysir, Abu Khadija, and Abu Hafs. A co-founder of Al Qaeda, this Egyptian terrorist, before he was killed in Afghanistan in the November 2001 bombing of Al Qaeda and Taliban strongholds, had been likely to assume the leadership of Al Qaeda if bin Laden had been killed or captured. Atef served as the head of the Military Committee. Authorities say that he played a leading role in the bombing of the U.S. Embassy in Nairobi in 1998. His daughter is married to one of bin Laden's sons.

(Courtesy FBI)

Muhammed Atef (killed in Afghanistan, November 2001).

- **Ayman al-Zawahiri,** a.k.a. the Doctor, Abu Muhammad, Abu Abdullah, Abu al-Mu-iz, the Teacher, Ustaz, Abdel Muaz, and Nur. A longtime leader in Egypt's Islamic Jihad terrorist group, this Cairo physician was among those charged with the 1981 assassination of Egyptian president Anwar Sadat and is a prime suspect in the attempted assassination of Hosni Mubarak, Sadat's successor, in Ethiopia. He, too, is a founding father of Al Qaeda and oversees the group's Islamic Study Committee. In December 2001 it was reported that his wife and children were killed and he was wounded in a U.S. air strike on Al Qaeda strongholds in Afghanistan. Al-Zawahiri is believed by the FBI to be the mastermind behind the September 11 attacks on the World Trade Center and the Pentagon.

(Courtesy FBI)

Ayman al-Zawahiri.

■ **Abdullah Ahmed Abdullah,** a.k.a. Saleh, Abu Mohammed el Masry, Abu Marium, and Abu Mohammad el
Masri Saas al Sharif. This seasoned
veteran of the Afghan war against
the Soviets tutored the *Mujahedeen*
(the Afghan rebels, some of whom
later became Al Qaeda leaders) in
the art of using explosives. An
Egyptian national of Saudi origin,
Abdullah was one of five indicted by
a U.S. grand jury on December 20,
2000, for the 1998 East African
Embassy bombings. He is a member
of both the Military and the Islamic
Study committees.

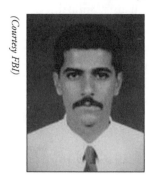

(Courtesy FBI)

*Abdullah Ahmed
Abdullah.*

(Courtesy FBI)

Anas al Liby.

■ **Anas al Liby,** a.k.a. Nazih al Raghie.
This Libyan national is a surveillance
expert who reconnoitered the U.S.
Embassy in Nairobi and taught
members of the group techniques
such as map reading, blueprinting,
measuring wall thickness, and
installing hidden cameras. He helped
draft the Al Qaeda manuals. Al Liby
was indicted on December 20, 2000,
by a U.S. grand jury on charges of
conspiracy to commit murder and to
destroy U.S. defense installations.

(Courtesy FBI)

Saif al Adel.

■ **Saif al Adel,** a.k.a. Saif. Little is
known about this member of the
Shura Council, but he served for
many years as a member of Egypt's
Islamic Jihad organization and was

fingered by the FBI as a key figure in the 1993 ambush of U.S. soldiers in Somalia.

Al-Fadl also mentioned two other Al Qaeda leaders as being members of the Shura Council:

- **Abu Ubaidah al Banshiri,** a.k.a. Aadil Habib, Galal Fouad Elmelify Abdeldaim, Jalal, and Adeel Habib. A co-founder of Al Qaeda, Banshiri was the emir of the Military Committee. He was a police officer in Egypt before he went to fight in the jihad against the Soviets in Afghanistan. According to CIA reports, al Banshiri drowned in a ferry accident on Lake Victoria in May 1996.

- **Mamdouh Mahmud Salim,** a.k.a. Abu Hajer. An Iraqi, Salim established links between Al Qaeda and terrorist groups in Iraq and Lebanon. He was arrested in Germany in September 1998 and is presently in custody at the Metropolitan Correctional Center in New York. According to FBI reports, Salim co-founded Al Qaeda and managed several camps and guesthouses in Afghanistan and Pakistan. In November 2000, he stabbed a prison guard in the eye, stabbed another in the stomach, and sprayed irritants on others during a failed prison escape.

The Military Committee is responsible for the recruitment of soldiers; training in small arms, artillery, and demolitions; and the purchase of weapons. An Islamic Study Committee ensures that all actions of the terrorist group are in complete conformity with the teachings of the Koran. The Finance Committee controls the group's income and expenses (al-Fadl was a paymaster). A media committee oversees the group's public relations, designed to obtain the support of all believers, and publishes the in-house newspaper, *Nashrat al-Akhbar.*

According to the information provided by Jamal Ahmed al-Fadl and other informants, Al Qaeda is structured in the following manner:

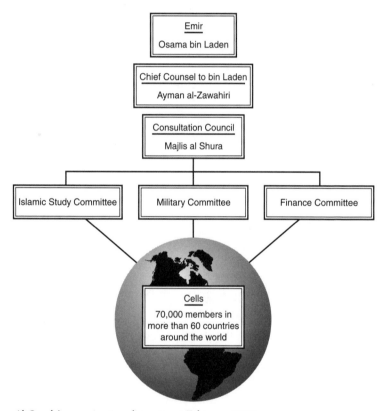

Al Qaeda's organizational structure, February 2001.

- **Emir.** Osama bin Laden.
- **Ayman al-Zawahiri.** The chief counsel to bin Laden, he was a co-founder of Al Qaeda. He is revered by the

group not only for his erudition and his profession as a physician but also because of his renowned career as a leader of Egyptian Islamic Jihad.

- **Shura, or Consultation Council.** This group of seasoned terrorists and confidants known as *majlis al shura* must approve major decisions such as terrorist attacks and the issuing of fatwas (edicts). The council members play leadership roles in the organization's major committees, made up of lower-ranking Al Qaeda members.
- **The Committees.**

  The Military Committee oversees recruitment, war training, and the purchase of arms.

  The Islamic Study Committee makes rulings on religious law and trains all recruits in the teachings of the Koran and jihad.

  The Finance Committee oversees corporate holdings, including the travel office and several other companies. Taba Investments engages in currency trading; another bin Laden international company engages in the import and export of goods; Thermar-al-Mirbaraka owns and operates farms throughout the Middle East that produce sesame and white corn; the Khartoum Tannery produces leather goods; Al Hijra is involved in major construction projects throughout the Middle East; the Qudarat Transport Company operates buses and a fleet of transport trucks; and there is the very lucrative narcotics business in Afghanistan. Bin Laden and his group also operate a chain of shops that sell top-grade Yemeni honey. Another source of income is tribute exacted from Middle Eastern states in exchange for bin Laden's promise not to set up Al Qaeda cells within their borders. This final source of income is akin to the Danegeld paid by Anglo-Saxon kings to Viking warriors.

■ **The Cells.** The network of terrorist recruitment and training has sites throughout the world. Each cell engages in missions independent of the others, and the members and activities of the other cells are kept secret. This typical pattern of state intelligence agencies safeguards the overall objectives of the organization.

■ **The Headquarters.** Al Qaeda's early base of operations was near the city of Peshawar in Pakistan. In 1991 the terrorist group relocated to Sudan and remained there until 1996. From Sudan, Al Qaeda returned to Afghanistan, where bin Laden issued the "Declaration of War Against the Americans Occupying the Land of the Two Holy Mosques." In May 1999 Al Qaeda moved to Farmihadda, Afghanistan, a few miles south of Jalalabad near the Pakistani border in an ex-military installation called Tora Bora, a place that became familiar to the world in the winter of 2001. In 1998 the Base moved from month to month through the terrorist training camps in eastern Afghanistan, including the Zhawar Kili Camp. As this book was going to press, the whereabouts of the Al Qaeda leadership were unknown.

Al Qaeda, al-Fadl maintained, also employed the services of Abu Muaz el-Masry, an interpreter of dreams. He attended all meetings of the committees and the Shura Council and met with bin Laden on a daily basis.

Al Qaeda Training

Jamal Ahmed al-Fadl's career as a terrorist ended in 1996, when he was banished from Al Qaeda for stealing. As he tells it, he had, indeed, stolen more than $100,000 of Al Qaeda funds, but only after he had complained to bin Laden several times about his salary (only a third of what his Egyptian counterparts were earning) and been told that they were worth more than him. He was so angry with bin Laden that he ran straight to the CIA and offered to tell investigators everything he knew, which was a great deal (and resulted in the conviction of four Al Qaeda members for the East African Embassy bombings).

As al-Fadl's terrorism career came to an end, Mohamed Rashed Daoud Al-'Owhali's career as an Al Qaeda suicide bomber was just getting underway. Mohamed is another informant. He, too, testified at the trial of the four Al Qaeda terrorists who were involved in the bombings of the U.S. embassies.

Al-'Owhali is 26, well spoken, and intense. He was born in Liverpool, England, and moved to Saudi Arabia, the homeland of his wealthy parents, when he was a young boy.

In Saudi Arabia, he became steeped in the teachings of Islam and attended a religious university in Riyadh. He read books about the Muslim martyrs and heard the speeches of the blind Egyptian Sheikh Omar Abd al-Rahman, who was convicted in 1995 for his role in a conspiracy to blow up New York City landmarks.

At age 21, Al-'Owhali entered the Zahwar Kal al-Badr camp, the first in a series of Al Qaeda training facilities he would attend in the Hindu Kush Mountains and the barren desert plains of Afghanistan. Several of the recruits were from New York and London, but most came, like Al-'Owhali, from religious schools called *madrasahs*. In Pakistan alone, more than 6,000 such schools had been established to uphold the principles of Islamic fundamentalism and the sacredness of jihad.

Typical recruits for Al Qaeda and its sister groups are unmarried males between ages 17 and 25. The terrorist organizations utilize the services of scouts—teachers in Muslim religious schools or the emirs of various mosques (such as Emir Mustafa Shalahi at the Farouq Mosque in New York)—to identify candidates suitable for training. The scouts usually choose youths who have been injured by ethnic conflict or who come from the dregs of Muslim society: those who have been victims of beatings, or who have lost a father or brother in a demonstration, or who are without much hope of escaping a life of grinding poverty.

The chosen recruits were divided into small groups, where they collectively pored over passages from the Koran and chanted religious slogans. To create a sense of belonging and mystical cohesion and to grant the recruits a distinct identity as members of a spiritual brotherhood, the members of the Islamic Study Committee instructed the group of new recruits to repeat and memorize certain passages from the Koran five times a day at prayer services. One such passage was "I will be patient until Patience is worn out from patience." Bin Laden and other emirs of the jihad believe that Allah has designated the right time for attacks, and all true believers must wait for the appointed hour.

Along with the religious instruction came intensive military training. The young men were conditioned to come together by the same mechanics that pull together a football team, a boy scout troop, or an army platoon. The coming together was sealed through blood initiations—rites of passage in which the young men cried out their loyalty to Allah, to the emir, and to one another. They took solemn oaths with daggers to their breasts. Following this initiation, they emerged as members of an elite and holy fraternity of suicide bombers.

The members of the fraternity acted in absolute secrecy. They were instructed not to inform their parents of their mission. On a conscious level, the parents never knew the fate that awaited their children once they entered a training camp.

When Al-'Owhali's training was completed, he was granted an audience with Emir bin Laden, who impressed upon him the sacred duty of serving Allah and killing the enemies of the true faith: Americans and Jews.

Special Operations Training

Afghanistan was in turmoil when Al-'Owhali finished his Al Qaeda training. The ethnic coalition government of Ahmad Shah Massood was facing a rebellion of Pashtuns, the majority population in Afghanistan. The fundamentalist Islamic militia challenging Massood's government was the Taliban, led by Mullah Mohammed Omar. Al-'Owhali fought with the Taliban, which ousted Massood's government in 1996, and then gained entry to Al Qaeda's top-tier jihad camp for training in intelligence management, kidnapping, and hijacking.

In preparation for special operations, Al-'Owhali received intensive training in special operations weapons. The Al Qaeda manual specifies "cold steel weapons (wire, knife, rod); poisons, pistols, and rifles; and explosives." He further received training in methods of physical and psychological torture. The manual outlines the following methods of psychological torture:

1. Isolating the brother socially, cutting him off from public life, placing him in solitary confinement, and denying him news and information in order to make him feel lonely.

2. Forbidding calling him by name, giving the brother a number, and calling him by that number in order to defeat his morale.

3. Threatening to summon his sister, mother, wife, or daughter and rape her.

4. Threatening to rape the brother himself.

5. Threatening to confiscate his possessions and to have him fired from his employment.

6. Threatening to cause him permanent physical disability or life imprisonment.

7. Offering the brother certain enticements (apartment, car, passport, scholarship, and so on).

8. Using harsh treatment, insults, and curses to defeat his morale.

Al-'Owhali completed his special operations training and was assigned to the Third Martyr's Barracks, First Squad, of the El Bara Bin Malik Division of the Army of Liberating the Islamic Holy Lands. He met with bin Laden several times and expressed his desire to perform a suicide mission against America as soon as possible in order to enter paradise and receive his reward of 72 *houris* (virgins), untouched by man or *jinn* (invisible spirits). Bin Laden responded by saying "Be patient. Take your time. Your mission will come."

The East Africa Mission

Soon the mission did come. Al-'Owhali was ordered to shave his beard and report to another terrorist cell in Yemen. His new commanders gave him a passport that identified him as an Iraqi named Abdul Ali Latif. In Yemen he received training in security and proper deportment while on a mission. Much of the training came from information contained in the Al Qaeda manual, such as the following list of standard Al Qaeda security precautions:

1. Keep the passport in a safe.
2. All documents of the undercover brother, such as identity cards and passport, should be falsified.
3. When the undercover brother is traveling with a certain identity card or passport, he should know all pertinent [information] such as the name, profession, and place of residence.
4. The brother who has special work status [commander, communication link] should have more than one identity card and passport. He should learn the contents of each, the nature of the [indicated] profession, and the dialect of the resident area listed in the document.
5. The photograph of the brother in these documents should be without a beard. It is preferable that the brother's public photograph [on these documents] also be without a beard.
6. When using identity documents in different names, no more than one such document should be carried at one time.

Al-'Owhali spent two years with other Al Qaeda camp graduates in Yemen, where he received a Yemeni passport and another name: Khalid Salim Saleh bin Rashid. During that time, he received training in security measures that must be observed by all Al Qaeda operatives on a mission.

The manual outlines the security measures to be followed when traveling on public transportation:

1. One should select public transportation that is not subject to frequent checking along the way, such as crowded trains or public buses.
2. Boarding should be done at a secondary station, as main stations undergo more careful surveillance.

3. The cover should match the general appearance (tourist bus, first-class train, second-class train, and so on).

4. The document used should support the cover.

5. Important luggage should be placed among the passengers' luggage without identifying who placed it. If it is discovered, its owner would not be arrested.

6. The brother traveling on a "special mission" should not get involved in religious issues or day-to-day matters.

7. The brother traveling on a mission should not arrive in the [destination] country at night because then travelers are few and there are [search] parties and check points along the way.

8. When cabs are used, conversation of any kind should not be started because many cab drivers work for security apparatus.

9. The brother should exercise extreme caution and apply all security measures to the other members.

From Yemen, Al-'Owhali was ordered to Pakistan, where a senior Al Qaeda leader told him that the mission for which he was chosen was glorious. He was headed for martyrdom and would assist in driving a truck full of explosives into an embassy of the enemy in East Africa.

Al-'Owhali was also told to make a martyrdom video that "would be played upon the successful completion of his mission."

His part in the mission was to ride in the passenger seat of the bomb truck. His partner, an equally committed member of Al Qaeda named Azzam, was to be the driver. At the gate of the U.S. Embassy in Nairobi, Al-'Owhali was to jump out of the truck, throw stun grenades at the entrance guard, lift the gate for the truck, and hop back in the vehicle for the ride to paradise. All went well. Al-'Owhali threw the grenades. He lifted the gate. He joined his companion in crashing the truck into the embassy. The bomb exploded. Azzam was blown to smithereens, but Al-'Owhali, to his eternal shame, was left with only cuts and bruises.

The crestfallen young soldier of the jihad ended up not in paradise, but in a U.S. military prison.

Al-'Owhali remains bitter. He says that he would like to die. But he adds, "To die after your mission is not martyrdom, but suicide." Suicide is taboo in Islam.

2

Muhammad, Islam, and the Koran

"Recite in the name of your Lord, who created man from clots of blood! Recite! Your Lord is the Most Bountiful One, who by the pen taught man what he did not know."
—The Koran (96:1–5) ["The Blood Clots"]

"Fight in the cause of Allah those who fight you, but do not transgress limits, for Allah does not love transgressors. And slay them wherever you catch them, and turn them out of where they have turned you out, for tumult and oppression are worse than slaughter."
—The Koran (2:190–191)

The Islamic faith is based on the life of Muhammad and the teachings of the Koran. Like all religions, it has given rise to a mainstream body of belief and ideological extremes. One extreme is represented by the ascetic Sufis, who live in monasteries and preach a doctrine of worldly renunciation and pacifism. Another extreme is represented by terrorist groups such as Al Qaeda, who live in military cells and preach a doctrine of military action and utopianism. The tensions within Islam are explained by the following passage from *The Economist* (September 20, 2001):

"Nearly all Muslims … think of jihad as striving to perfect oneself, or to give hope to others by good example.
In short, they get on with their lives much like anyone
else. When the faith is under threat, however, some may
be inspired to go further—to fight to expel crusaders
from Palestine, say, as Muslims did in the thirteenth century, or to kick Russians out of Afghanistan, as they did
in the 1980s. A few may go to greater extremes. Some,
for example, follow the teachings of a fourteenth-century
firebrand, Ibn Taymiyya, who stated unequivocally,
'Jihad against the disbelievers is the most noble of
actions.' And some of these, a tiny radical minority, may
go so far as to plot carefully, and execute fearlessly, a suicidal slaughter of thousands of innocents in the name of
Allah."

In all of Osama bin Laden's edicts, interviews, and videotaped
messages and throughout Al Qaeda's manual, passages from the
Koran and incidents in the life of Muhammad are presented as
evidence that the group's violent acts are in accordance with the
teachings of the Koran and the Prophet's example. The killing of
innocent civilians, they say, is a means of serving God just as
surely as is their recitation of the prescribed prayers. Their political ideology is forged by their religious beliefs. In a 1999 interview with *Newsweek,* Osama bin Laden said "The terrorism we
practice is of the commendable kind for it is directed at the
tyrants and aggressors and the enemies of Allah."

Some informed observers believe that the terrorists are sin-
cere in their belief that the Koran compels them to wage war on
apostates and infidels. Others see bin Laden's use of the Koran as
the misuse of the words of the Prophet, words that he knew

would swell the ranks of Al Qaeda with men willing to die for his cause—the destruction of corrupt Muslim governments, and of the United States, the country whose troops are based near the holy cities of Mecca and Medina, and whose government supports Israeli rule over Jerusalem's Al Aqsa Mosque.

There is a great range of perspectives on the meaning of the Koran, colored by social and political forces that are as varied as the societies in which the world's Muslims live.

We'll return to the relationship between Islam and militant Islamic terrorism and offer different perspectives on it throughout this book. This chapter introduces the basics about the Prophet Muhammad, the faith of Islam, and the Koran.

The Youth of Muhammad

The Prophet Muhammad was born in Mecca (in what is now Saudi Arabia) in 570 C.E. Mecca was the holiest city in the Arab world. It was—and is—the site of the sacred shrine, the Kaaba, located near the miraculous spring of Zamzam, a square-shaped structure that contained the precious Black Stone that may have been a meteorite (*Kaaba* means "cube"). The shrine was dedicated to Allah, the high god of the Arab pantheon. The Arabs, at the time of Muhammad's birth, were polytheists, and the shrine was surrounded by 360 idols that might have represented the totems of the various tribes. Around the Kaaba was a circular area where pilgrims performed the ceremony of the *tawwaf*, the seven ritual circumambulations that traced the direction of the sun. The land around Mecca—20 miles in all directions—was, and is today, considered a safe haven, a place where all violence and fighting was prohibited.

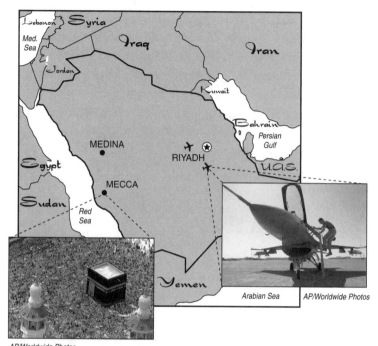

AP/Worldwide Photos

Mecca and the Kaaba (left) and U.S. bases in Saudi Arabia (right).

Once a year, Arabs were expected to travel to Mecca to make the circumambulations around the Kaaba; the yearly pilgrimages became known as the *hajj* (pilgrimage). For this reason, the desert city became a center of trade and commerce.

The richest tribesmen of Mecca were the Quraish. The Hashim, a clan within the Quraish tribe, had discovered the sacred spring of Zamzam and maintained the sole right to give its holy water to the pilgrims who made the hajj.

The Hashim clan was known for the handsomeness of its men. The most handsome and noble of the Hashim were the sons of Abdul Muttalib, whose youngest son Abdallah was the father of Muhammad.

Abdallah died of unknown causes while his wife Amina was pregnant. On the day her son was born, Amina sent for Abdul Muttalib, her deceased husband's father, and told him that she had received a revelation that the newborn baby would be "a light for the Arab people." The grandfather took his newly born grandson to the Kaaba and named him Muhammad, or "the Praised One."

As was the custom of the Quraish tribe at that time, Amina gave her baby to a woman from one of the Bedouin tribes so he could be nursed in the open air of the desert.

When Muhammad was returned to his mother at the age of five, she took him on a journey to Yathrib. She died on the way back to Mecca, and Muhammad came into the care of his uncle, Abu Talib, the chief of the Hashim clan.

Nothing seems to be unusual about Muhammad's early life. Occasionally, we are told, he traveled with his uncle on caravans to Damascus and other cities. But no miracles took place; no epiphanies occurred. Among his clansmen, Muhammad became known as Al-Amin, "the reliable one," because of his ability to perform his duties in a timely manner and inspire confidence in others.

At age 25, Muhammad became employed by the rich widow, Khadijah, who lived in Mecca. She was so impressed by his dependable and conscientious work that she offered to marry him. Even though Muhammad was 15 years younger than Khadijah, he accepted and was deeply devoted to her. As long as Khadijah lived, Muhammad took no other wife.

Khadijah bore Muhammad four daughters and two sons; the sons died in infancy. The couple also adopted Ali, the orphan son of Muhammad's beloved uncle Abu Talib. Ali later married Fatima, who provides this description of Muhammad at age 45:

"He was of middle stature, neither tall nor short. His complexion was rosy white; his eyes black; his hair—thick, brilliant, and beautiful—fell to his shoulders. His profuse beard fell to his breast .... There was such sweetness in his visage that no one, once in his presence, could leave him. If I hungered, a single look at the Prophet's face dispelled the hunger. Before him all forgot their grief and pains."

Very few details are known about Muhammad's life, so it is only by inference that scholars have been able to shed light on the evolution of Muhammad the caravan leader into Muhammad the Prophet of a new monotheistic religion. In Mecca he met several Christians, including Khadijah's cousin Waraqah ibn Nawfal. His travels with the caravans frequently took him to Yathrib, where his father had died and where Jews constituted a large part of the population. He also came into contact with the Quraish oligarchy of Mecca and with the unenfranchised of many different tribes who worshipped various gods. Over a period of years his encounters, combined with his contemplative nature, developed in him both a growing commitment to monotheism and the impetus to address the social disparities of the time.

Muhammad Becomes the Prophet

It is known that Muhammad frequently retreated to a cave at the foot of Mount Herra, three miles from Mecca, to spend several days and nights in contemplation and meditation. He was 40 when, on one of his customary visits to the cave, the pivotal moment in the history of Islam took place. Muhammad related the event as follows to his chief biographer, Muhammad Ibn Ishaq:

"While I was asleep, with a coverlet of silk brocade whereon was some writing, the angel Gabriel appeared to me and said, 'Read!' I said, 'I do not read.' He pressed me with the coverlets so tightly that I thought I was near death. Then he let me go and said, 'Read!' So I read aloud. And he departed from me at last. And I awoke from my sleep, and it was as though these words were written on my heart. I went forth, until, when I was midway on the mountain, I heard a voice from heaven saying, 'O Muhammad! You are the messenger of Allah, and I am Gabriel.' I raised my head toward heaven to see, and, lo, Gabriel in the form of a man with his feet set evenly on the rim of the sky was saying: 'O Muhammad! You are the messenger of Allah, and I am Gabriel.'"

Since the encounter was both violent and accompanied by convulsions that sent him into a state of unconsciousness, Muhammad was unsure of the source of his vision. He feared that he might be possessed by one of the jinn that commonly inhabited the souls of Arab poets and soothsayers.

When he returned home, Khadijah, along with her Christian cousin Waraqah, convinced Muhammad that he had received a true revelation from the true God. Emboldened, he began to preach about his vision of one God and about the need to resolve the social inequities between the nepotistic ruling tribes and the common folk.

Muhammad, according to Islamic tradition, could neither read nor write. For this reason, he is called the "*ummi* [unlettered] prophet." This is significant because Muhammad recited the Koran to his followers who, in turn, recited the teachings to new converts. (The word *Koran* comes from the Arabic *qaraa*, meaning "to recite.")

During this period a patchwork of tribes roamed the Arabian Peninsula, governed by rules of kinship. The Quraish, who held sway in Mecca, were attempting to bring the tribes together under a centralized authority. When Muhammad arrived in Mecca to preach social unity and solidarity based on Islam, the idea already had some currency. The injustices of the ruling Quraish provided him with ready converts to his message: Submit to one God—Allah.

At the Kaaba in Mecca, Muhammad, who continued to receive visions, preached the doctrine of one god to all the merchants, pilgrims, and tribesmen and proclaimed himself to be a true prophet. He spoke of the resurrection of the dead, the final judgment, and the need of the populace to *submit* or *surrender* to the will of Allah. The word *Islam* is the infinitive of the Arabic for "submit" or "surrender," and *Muslim* is the present participle of the same infinitive. A Muslim is one who submits. The Muslim world is divided between those who submit and those who fail to submit. Failure to submit, however, does not necessarily close the path to Allah. Muslims recognize Abraham, Moses, and Jesus as prophets, and they consider Muhammad to be the final prophet sent by Allah/God. Jews and Christians ("the People of the Book" [*Ahl al Kitab*]), considered to be on the wrong path because of the corruption of their holy books, have always been urged to surrender to Islam but have been tolerated if they did not do so.

The Prophet opened his house to all who would hear him—rich and poor, Jew and Christian, slave and free man, Arab and non-Arab. His impassioned words moved some to belief. His first convert was his aging wife Khadijah; his second, his cousin and foster son Ali; the third, his servant Zaid, whom he had bought as a slave and immediately freed; and the fourth, his kinsman Abu Bakr, a man of high standing among the Quraish. Abu Bakr brought to the new faith five other leading tribesmen of Mecca.

Abu Bakr and these men became the Prophet's six "Companions," whose memories of him would come to constitute the most revered traditions of Islam.

The Hijra: The Birth of Islam

Muhammad's message of monotheism was threatening to the financial interests of Mecca's Quraish merchant class, who profited from pilgrimages of polytheists to the Kaaba. Hostility between Muhammad and the merchants intensified to the point where he was warned by his uncle that his life was in danger. So the Prophet and his followers fled to Yathrib. His flight from Mecca on July 16, 622 C.E., is known to all Muslims as the *Hijra;* it marks the beginning of the Muslim religion. Yathrib later came to be called Medina ("the city") to designate Muhammad's association with it. It is the second most sacred place in Islam.

Because the Hijra was the beginning of Islam, the Islamic calendar is calibrated to it. In Islamic chronology, 632 C.E., the year of Muhammad's death, is designated as 10 A.H., and the year 2002 C.E. is designated as 1380 A.H.

Before Muhammad went from Mecca to Medina, he received a vision in which he was transported in his sleep to Jerusalem, where a winged horse, Buraq, awaited him at the Wailing Wall, the ruins of the Jewish Temple. Mounting Buraq, Muhammad flew to heaven and back again. By a miracle, the Prophet awoke to find himself safe in bed. The legend of this flight made Jerusalem the third holy city of Islam.

At Medina, a city torn by tribal feuding, Muhammad experienced great success as a statesman, legislator, and judge—the head of state of a new and thriving theocracy. In order to become

a member of this community of believers, an Arab was expected
to make his own hijra—to leave his tribe and join the *Ummah*
(Muslim community) of Medina. This requirement is contained
in the following teaching from the Koran:

> "Those who believed and made the hijra and struggled
> with possessions and persons in the way of God, and
> those who gave their homes and helped, these are the
> protectors of one another. To those who believe but did
> not make the hijra, it is not for you to give protection
> until they do make the hijra. If they ask you for help in
> respect for religion, it is your duty to give help, unless it
> is against a tribe with whom you have a treaty." (8:72)

At first, there was harmony between the Jews of Medina, a sizeable portion of the populace, and the newly arrived Muslims.
The Jews found similarities between the teachings of the Prophet
and their own beliefs, including the doctrine of monotheism, the
concept of a prophet as a divine messenger, and the belief in the
resurrection of the body and the Last Judgment. The closeness
between the two religious bodies was evidenced in a mosque
built in April 623, seven months after the Hijra. The northern
wall faced Jerusalem and bore a small niche (called the *qiblah*)
that designated the Holy City of the Jews, which was also the setting of the Prophet's dream—the Buraq—as the place to which
all Muslims should turn in prayer. To summon the Muslims to
prayer, Muhammad thought of using a ram's horn as the Jews did
but he later decided to have a disciple with an especially resonant
voice climb a high tower and cry out *"Allahu akbar"* ("God is the
greatest") to the people of the city.

The good relations between Muslims and Jews, however,
gradually began to deteriorate. Caesar E. Farah, in his book,
Islam, says that the Jews, after "two years of theological debate

with the new prophet became convinced that he was not exactly the Messiah they had been awaiting." The Qaynuqa' Jews, according to the Prophet's biographer Ibn Ishaq (surah 4), began to gather at the mosque before services to "listen to the stories of the Muslims and scoff at their religion."

Muhammad's early vision of accommodating Jewish beliefs and practices in Islam grew dimmer as hostilities increased, and in January 624, 18 months after the Hijra, he made a dramatic change in Muslim worship. He instructed his people to turn in prayer, not to Jerusalem, but to Mecca. This change in the qiblah represented a change in attitude toward the Jews and anticipated the assertion of a new Muslim identity.

As opposition from the Jews mounted, antagonism grew between the Quraish and Muhammad and his followers, who were routinely conducting raids (*ghazis*) on caravans that traveled to Mecca. At the time, raids, as Karen Armstrong points out in her biography of the Prophet, were almost a national sport. In the case of Muhammad and his impoverished Muslim followers, they were more a necessity due to economic hardship.

During the same month that the qiblah was changed to Mecca, in an attempt to put an end to Muslim raids, the Quraish leaders set out from Mecca with an army of 900 soldiers to attack Muhammad and his band of 300 raiders. The attack took place at Wadi Badr, 30 miles from Medina. The Quraish fought in the old tribal style, with reckless bravado and a chief leading each clan, so that the army lacked a unified command. But the Muslims under Muhammad were strictly disciplined and fought in tight formation. By the middle of the day, the Quraish, who thought they would defeat the Muslims by a mere show of force, panicked and fled in disarray into the desert, leaving hundreds of soldiers and more than 50 of the tribe's leaders dead in the field. The Muslims were elated.

The Battle of Badr was a great victory for the Prophet. For years, he had been ridiculed and scorned by the leaders of Mecca and the Bedouin tribes. But his great military victory—against all odds—over the most powerful Arab tribe made him a revered and respected figure throughout the Arabian Peninsula. People listened to his message with new interest.

A few days later, Muhammad ordered the Muslims to fast during the month of Ramadan to commemorate the triumph at Badr. This fast (*Saum*), which was first observed in March 625, became one of the Five Pillars of Islam.

The following year, the Quraish returned with a massive force. Medina's three major Jewish tribes, who had mutual assistance pacts with the Muslims, defaulted on their agreements. Muhammad's followers were defeated. The Prophet himself was nearly killed, but the Meccan invaders did not venture to enter Medina.

As if that were not enough, the Qaynuqa' Jews taunted the Muslims about their lack of skill in battle. In response, Muhammad assembled his troops and blockaded them in their quarters without food or water. Several days later, after listening to their cries for mercy, he permitted them to depart from the city, with the proviso that they leave all of their possessions behind.

This was a dangerous time for Muhammad. He knew that another attack would be coming from Mecca. Many of his men had deserted under fire, and the remainder of his followers were disheartened and in disarray.

The attack from the Quraish came in March 627, when an army of 10,000 set out from Mecca to conquer the Ummah at Medina. In preparation, Muhammad and his men dug a huge trench around the desert city. The soil from the trench was used to construct a high escarpment to raise the Muslim defenders above their attackers. The Quraish army stopped before the trench, only to be met by a shower of arrows and spears. On the few occasions when Quraish horsemen managed to make it across the trench, they were hacked to pieces by Muslim swords. The rout was complete. By the end of the day, the Prophet stood as the most powerful tribal leader in Arabia.

Following the triumph, Muhammad was informed that the Jewish tribe of the Bani Qurayzah, with whom the Muslims had a pact, had planned to grant the Quraish army access through their fortifications. The Prophet responded by ordering the execution of 900 Jewish men and the sale of their women and children into slavery.

> In her discussion of the massacre of the Jews of the Bani Qurayzah, Karen Armstrong writes:
>
> "The massacre of Qurayzah is a reminder of the desperate conditions of Arabia during Muhammad's lifetime. Of course we are right to condemn it without reserve, but it was not as great a crime as it would be today. Muhammad was not working within a world empire which imposed widespread order nor within one of the established religious traditions. He had nothing like the Ten Commandments (though even Moses is said to have commanded the Israelites to massacre the entire population of Canaan shortly after he had told them: 'Thou shalt not kill'). All Muhammad had was the old tribal morality which had permitted this expedient to preserve the group. The problem was compounded by the fact that Muhammad's victory had made him the most powerful chief in Arabia at the head of a group that was not a conventional tribe. He had just begun to transcend tribalism and was in a no man's land between two stages of social development."

Mecca Becomes Islam's Holy City

Mecca now became the focal point of the new faith. Enlisting the help of nomadic Arab tribes, Muhammad led a series of armed raids on Mecca, and in 630 C.E. captured the city with no resistance. The Prophet responded magnanimously by declaring a general amnesty for all but a few of his enemies. He destroyed the idols in the Kaaba and proclaimed it a mosque. He spared the Black Stone and sanctioned the practice of kissing it. He pronounced Mecca to be the holy city of Islam and decreed that no unbeliever should ever set foot on its sacred soil. Many pagans converted to Islam.

Muhammad lived a life of unassuming simplicity. He lived not in the Great Mosque, but in a simple cottage, 12 feet square, 8 feet high, and thatched with palm leaves. His furniture consisted of a mattress and pillows on the ground. He mended his own clothes, swept his own floor, and milked the family goat. Despite all the revenue and booty that came to him, Muhammad spent little on his family and even less on himself. He gave almost all of his money to the poor and needy.

The remaining years of the Prophet's life were spent in triumph as the various Arabian tribes became united under the banner of Islam. His last words to his followers were as follows:

> "Know that every Muslim is a Muslim's brother and that all Muslims are brethren, fighting between them should be avoided, and the bloodshed in ancient days should be avenged, Muslims should fight all other men until they say, 'There is no God but Allah.'"

The Koran

> "By the declining star, your compatriot is not in error, nor is he deceived! He does not speak out of his own

fancy. This is the inspired revelation. He is taught by the one who is powerful and mighty. He stood on the uppermost horizon; then, drawing near, he came down within two bows' length or even closer and revealed to his servant that which he revealed. His own heart did not deny his vision."

—The Koran (53:1–11)

"Recite!" This was the command from the angel Gabriel to the Prophet Muhammad. Muhammad was ordered to repeat the words from the holy book that had been penned by Allah and was kept in heaven. These recitations were collected after the Prophet's death and compiled in the Koran.

Consisting of 114 chapters called surahs, the Koran is a nonchronological book of verses. Each verse reflects a different period in the life of the Prophet. Each surah is divided into verses or *ayah*. The Arabic ayah carries with it the meaning of a miracle. For those seeking the validity of Muhammad's calling, the Prophet would maintain that the Koran itself represented a miraculous confirmation of it.

The surahs, with the exception of the short *fatihah* (opening chapter), are arranged from the longest to the shortest. Each surah is introduced by the formulaic verse, the *basmalah* ("In the name of God, the Merciful, the Compassionate"). This verse begins every Muslim prayer and is spoken by pious Muslims (including Osama bin Laden and his terrorists) at the start of every important activity. The basmalah is invoked by travelers before departure, athletes before a competition, and married people before intercourse. The words are printed at the beginning of religious texts (including the Al Qaeda manual) and are spoken before every meal, every political speech, and every press announcement.

After the death of Muhammad, the individual surahs existed only in a completely chaotic condition. Some were recorded on stone tablets and wood; others on bones and fragments of clothing. Finally, in 652 C.E., the third *caliph*, Uthman, ordered the scattered texts to be gathered together and edited.

The language of the Koran is Arabic, and because it was given by Allah to Muhammad in Arabic and exists in heaven in Arabic, for centuries it was considered blasphemous to translate its 6,239 surahs into any other language. Today there are unauthorized translations in 43 languages, and there are even a few official ones.

The Tenets of Islam

There are seven basic beliefs in Islam. Muslims must accept monotheism, jinn (angels and demons), the revealed books of Allah, the prophets, accountability for their actions, divine judgment, and resurrection.

Monotheism. Pre-Islamic Arabs were divided into factions that waged war on one another because they were polytheists and failed to realize the oneness of God. This realization of the one God, Allah, is the most important revelation Muhammad received from the angel Gabriel. The Koran devotes an entire surah (112) to this theme. The oneness of God is the teaching that Muslim *muazzin* (those who call people to prayer) chant several times a day atop thousands of minarets throughout the Islamic world. Worshipping or attributing deity to any other being but Allah is *shirk* (blasphemy). Allah, according to the tenets of Islam, is the source of all life, all growth, and all the blessings of the earth.

Angels and demons (jinn). Muslims believe in a well-structured organization of celestial and demonic beings. At the lowest level in the hierarchy of spiritual entities are the jinn, who were made out of fire. Unlike the angels, they eat, drink, copulate, and die. Some are good and heed the teachings of the Koran, but most are evil and spend their time tempting men and women to perform nasty deeds. The leader of the evil jinn is *Iblis* (Satan), who was once a great angel but was condemned for refusing to pay homage to Adam.

The angels of God in Islamic belief serve as Allah's secretaries and messengers. They are above the jinn in rank and distinction. Muslims believe that they are accompanied throughout life by a pair of angels, one on the right side and the other on the left, who record, respectively, their good and bad deeds.

Since Allah is all-knowing and the angels are all-recording, devout Muslims are scrupulous in what they say or do. They will not mention the names of Allah and the Prophet without giving them praise and glory and acknowledging their authority over their lives.

Allah's holy books. The Koran, as it was penned by Allah and kept for untold eons in heaven, is the most sacred of all texts— the Mother of All Books (*umm al-Kitab*). But the people of Islam accept other texts as sacred, including the Torah (the first five books of the Old Testament), the Davidic Psalms, and the Gospel (*Injil*) given to Jesus.

The prophets. Muslims believe that there has been a long succession of prophets through whom Allah has revealed his will, including Abraham (*Ibrahim*), Moses (*Musa*), and Jesus (*Isa*). Muhammad represents the culmination of all the earlier prophets and the last in the line. As proof of the finality of his revelation, Muhammad bore "the seal of the Prophet" on his body. This seal, located below one shoulder, was a birthmark "as large as a silver coin and surrounded by hairs."

Accountability, resurrection, and judgment. Similar to the teachings of Christian eschatology, Muslims believe in the resurrection of the body at the end of time. Only Allah knows when the end will come, but certain signs will signal its arrival. In the final days, faith in the true religion will have declined; morals will be loosened into chaotic permissiveness; and tumults and great wars will take place. Before the end comes, wise men will wish themselves dead. The final sign will be three blasts of the trumpet. At the first blast, the sun will go out, the stars will fall, the heavens will melt, all tall buildings and mountains will be leveled, and the sea will dry out and burst into flames. At the second blast, living creatures, jinn, angels, and men will be annihilated—except the favored few of Allah. They will inhabit the earth until Israfel, the angel of music, blows the third and last blast. When that happens, the dead will rise from their graves and Allah will come down from heaven. A final judgment will take place. The wicked and the infidels will fall into the pits of hell, and the good and the righteous will pass over into Paradise.

> Paradise, particularly for martyrs, is really heaven. It consists of one vast garden, watered by peaceful streams and shaded with spreading fruit trees. Martyrs will be dressed in silk robes and will be served by handsome attendants. They will drink wine (forbidden on Earth) and never suffer a hangover. In addition, every martyr will be granted 72 houris (virgins) as a reward. These maidens "with swelling breasts and modest gaze" will cater to every desire of the blessed.

The Five Pillars

There are five basic rituals, reflecting Islam's beliefs, that Muslims perform in daily life. They are called the Five Pillars.

Creed. The first pillar of Islam is the profession of faith, known as the *Shahadah,* that every Muslim must recite every day. *"Ashhadu an la ilaha illa Llah, wa ashhadu anna Muhammad rasulu Llah"* ("I testify that there is no God but Allah, and I testify that Muhammad is his prophet"). These words are whispered into the ears of newborn infants and are spoken by the dying before they pass over into Paradise. They are recited in times of crisis and intoned to give weight to official announcements. As the most basic creed of Islam, the words are found in all mosques and all religious amulets. A non-Muslim who repeats these words three times in the presence of Muslim witnesses testifies to his or her conversion to Islam—a step that can never be revoked.

Prayer. The *Salat* (prayer for intercession and a desire for blessing) must be repeated by all Muslims several times a day: between dawn and sunrise, at noon, in mid-afternoon, after sundown, and before going to bed. In order for the prayer to be valid, the location where the prayer is recited, the person's clothing, and the person must be clean. This involves ritual washing of the hands, forearms, head, and feet; rinsing out of the mouth; blowing out of the nose; and scrubbing of the ears. In order to achieve cleanliness of location, Muslims cover the ground with a prayer rug. They then pray facing Mecca.

Almsgiving. The third pillar of faith is the duty of Muslims to share their possessions with fellow believers. In Pakistan and Afghanistan, these alms, known as the *Zakat,* or holy tax, are used to support social and educational programs.

Fasting. During the 30 days of Ramadan, all Muslims are obliged to engage in ritual fasting (*Saum*). From early morning before sunrise until after sundown, they may neither eat nor drink. Members of Al Qaeda and other fundamentalist groups eat only a few dates and drink only water when the fast is broken after sundown. This practice is based on the following teaching:

"In the month of Ramadan, the Koran was revealed, a book of guidance with proofs of guidance distinguishing right from wrong. Therefore whoever of you is present in that month, let him fast .... Eat and drink until you can distinguish a white thread from a black one in the light of the coming dawn. Then resume the fast until night-fall."

—The Koran (2:185–187)

Pilgrimage to Mecca. The fifth pillar is the mandatory pilgrimage to Mecca, the "Mother of All Cities." All Muslims, including women, are supposed to make the journey to the center of the Islamic world at least once in their lifetime. Two forms of pilgrimage are possible. One is the "small" pilgrimage or *umrah* that is undertaken personally and is not bound by specific dates. This type of pilgrimage is not sufficient for the extremely pious. They commit to taking a "great" pilgrimage, or *hajj*, that can be undertaken only during the last month of the Islamic moon calendar and must be made in the company of other believers.

For the pilgrimage to be effective, pilgrims must be in a special state of consecration called *ihram*. They are forbidden to shave, comb their hair, use perfume or deodorant, or cut their hair or nails. In addition, they must remove their usual clothing and wear special robes when they reach the borders of the *haram*, the most sacred strip of land in all creation.

To understand Islam, one must come to terms not only with the life of the Prophet and the teachings of the Koran but with what is covered in the following chapter: the lives of the four "rightly guided" caliphs, the emergence of the schools of law, and a struggle for power that, still today, continues to divide Muslim from Muslim, Iraq from Iran, and terrorist from terrorist.

3

Islam's Sects and Struggles

"And don't be like those ... who split up their religion
and became mere sects, each rejoicing in what it claims
it has."
—The Koran (30:31–32)

The Prophet Muhammad had no sons, nor did he appoint a successor. After his death, his followers gathered to elect a leader and
to establish the polity for the religious community (Ummah).
Some argued that the ummah should not have a central government. They held that each tribe should have the right to elect its
own *imam*, or leader. But others insisted that Islam must be a
united community of believers with a single chief deputy or
caliph (from the Arabic *khalifah*, meaning "successor" or "representative"). After a heated debate, the proponents of a caliphate
held sway.

The next concern was the choice of a caliph. Some argued
that the leader should be a blood relative of the Prophet. Some
said that the caliph should come from the Medina converts. Still
others maintained that the successor of the Prophet must be one
of Muhammad's oldest and closest disciples. Eventually, this last
opinion prevailed, and Abu Bakr became the first caliph of
Islam.

Abu Bakr seemed to be the perfect choice. He was one of the Prophet's oldest and closest disciples. What's more, the new caliph was the father of Aisha, one of Muhammad's favorite wives. But not all Muslims accepted his rule. Abu Bakr was plagued with the problem of apostasy (*riddah*). Various Bedouin tribes elected their own religious leaders, refused to pay the obligatory *zakat* (annual donation) to Mecca, and began to conduct raids against the Muslims in Medina.

The caliph took decisive action. In a series of skirmishes called "the riddah wars," Abu Bakr was able to suppress rebellion and unify the tribes under the banner of Islam.

Abu Bakr not only united the tribes, he also forged them into a formidable military power. By 633, one year after his election, his troops had conquered Palestine and the Transjordan.

The Rightly Guided Caliphs

Abu Bakr is the first successor of Muhammad, the first leader of Islam. He and all his successors became known as caliphs; the first four, pious men, are called the "rightly guided" (*rashidun*) caliphs.

Abu Bakr's reign lasted only two years, and he was succeeded by Umar, under whom the Islamic expansion continued at an incredible pace. In 635, Damascus was taken; in 636, Antioch; in 638, Jerusalem. By 640, all of Syria was in Muslim hands; by 641, all of Persia and Egypt.

Within two decades of the death of Muhammad, the rule of the House of Islam extended from North Africa to the Caucasus; and in the east, beyond Iran from the Oxus River (Amu Darya) to present-day Afghanistan.

The Muslim triumph, as Karen Armstrong points out in her book *Islam: A Short History,* is one of the great phenomena of world history:

"Before the coming of Islam, the Arabs had been a despised outgroup; but in a remarkably short space of time they had inflicted major defeats upon two world empires. The experience of conquest enhanced their sense that something tremendous had happened to them. Membership of the ummah was thus a transcendent experience, because it went beyond anything they had known or could have imagined in the old tribal days. Their success also endorsed the message of the Koran, which had asserted that a correctly guided society must prosper because it was in tune with God's laws."

The spirit of exhilaration was dampened in 644, when Umar was stabbed in the mosque of Medina by a Persian prisoner of war who had a personal grievance against him.

The third legitimate caliph was an old man named Uthman. Under his rule, the conquests continued into Libya in the west and the Indian subcontinent in the east. But the caliph created dissention when he appointed his Umayyad kinsmen to every key political position. Complaints about nepotism and corruption abounded throughout the Muslim Empire. In 656 a group of Egyptian Muslims stormed the imperial palace in Medina and killed Uthman as he sat reading the Koran.

After Uthman's murder, Ali, the Prophet's son-in-law, became the fourth and last legitimate caliph. Ali's appointment was opposed by two factions. One faction was led by Talhah and Zubayr, two early converts, who received the support of Muhammad's aging wife Aisha. The second faction was led by

Muawiyah, a member of the Umayyad tribe who claimed to be the rightful successor to Uthman.

In 656 Ali defeated both factions at the Battle of the Camel in southeastern Mesopotamia. Five years later, the victorious Ali was stabbed in the back by a disgruntled tribesman. This event precipitated the great division within Islam.

Muslims would later define themselves and their theology in accordance with the way they assessed the turbulent, triumphant, and tragic events of these early years.

Following Ali's murder, Muawiyah assumed the caliphate, but not without opposition from Ali's supporters, who became known as *Shi'as* (from the Arabic *shi'at Ali,* "the partisans of Ali"). They maintained that a caliph must be a direct descendant of the Prophet. The partisans of Ali rejected Muawiyah and named Hasan, the son of Ali and Fatima, as their caliph, and placed him on a throne in Kafa in modern Syria. Muawiyah reacted with righteous wrath. He summoned an army and marched upon Kafa. Hasan offered no opposition. He relinquished his title and pledged allegiance to Muawiyah. In return, Hasan received a pension from the Umayyad tribe and was allowed to return to Mecca, where (so it's said) he married 100 women and died at age 45.

In 680 Muawiyah was succeeded by his son, Yezid. This resulted in another attempt by the Shi'as to seize power. They offered the caliphate to Hussein, the younger brother of Hasan, and summoned him to Kafa to rejoin the struggle to end the Umayyad dynasty once and for all. Hussein accepted the invitation and set out from Mecca with his family and a band of faithful followers. Twenty-five miles from Kafa, Yezid's army attacked Hussein's caravan and put him to the sword, along with his sons, brothers, cousins, and nephews.

Karbala, the site of this massacre, remains a sacred pilgrimage place for Shi'as. Every year, Shi'a Muslims hold passion plays to commemorate the martyrdom of Hussein. Many go to extremes, slicing open their foreheads with sharp blades and beating themselves with barbed whips to express their sorrow over the cruel murder. What happened 1,400 years ago is just as pressing and meaningful to such believers as events that occurred in recent history.

But the Shi'as' struggle against the Umayyad dynasty was continued by Abdallah, a distant relative of Muhammad. In 683 Yezid, with a Syrian army, laid siege to Abdallah and his Shi'a supporters in Mecca. The rocks from the catapults of Yezid's army smashed the sacred mosque and split the sacred Black Stone in three places. The structure that supported the Kaaba caught fire and burned to the ground. The rebellion, for the time being, was over, and the great monolithic structure of Islam, like the Black Stone, fell into three factions.

Sunnis, Shi'as, and Sufis

The first and by far the largest group remained the Sunnis, who would rule over the "golden age" of Islam. About 80 percent of all Muslims are members of this branch. They hold that the caliph should belong to Muhammad's tribe, the Quraish, and that the Muslim community should choose him by consensus. Because Muhammad bore the "seal of the prophet," the Sunnis consider the responsibilities of the caliph merely to guard, not to continue, the prophetic legacy, and to oversee all Islamic affairs in accordance with the Koran and the *Shari'ah,* the body of laws that regulates Muslim life. The Sunnis believe that the *Sunnah* (way of behavior) of the first four caliphs, together with that of the Prophet, is authoritative for all believers.

The Shi'a branch of Islam claims about 20 percent of the Muslim population. Shi'as believe that the caliph should descend directly from the Prophet to Ali, Muhammad's son-in-law, and the last legitimate caliph. Unlike the Sunnis, their belief is that the Islamic leader (*imam*), is more than a mere guardian of Muhammad's prophetic legacy. They assert that Muhammad bequeathed to Ali and his successors his *wilaya* (spiritual authority), and that it enables the imams to interpret the Koran and lead the Islamic people in a manner that is infallible. The majority faction within the Shi'a branch, known as the Imamis (most of whom live in Iran), believe that the completion of the wilaya cycle will end with the messianic return of the twelfth imam, who has been hiding in heaven since the third century of Islam. The Imamis are certain that the *Ayatullahs* (senior experts in Islamic law) are able to communicate with the hidden Imam and, therefore, have the right to interpret Islamic law and make religious rulings.

The Sufi sect of Islam represents less than 1 percent of the Muslim community. Sufis interpret the Koran not as a political book, but a mystical one, which encourages withdrawal from the world. They seek union with Allah through absolute faith (*tawwakul*), strict asceticism (abstaining from food and earthly pleasures), and quiet meditation. Their meditation involves the recitation of certain names and formulas accompanied by rhythmic movements. Sufis are so named because they are expected to wear woolen robes (*suf* is Arabic for "wool").

Under the Umayyad dynasty (661–750), Islam expanded in all directions from China to France. Islamic learning flourished, and two schools of Islamic law (the Hanafites and the Malikites) were established. Free public hospitals and schools were set up in

Muslim cities, and Muslim scientists busied themselves making new discoveries.

After a series of wars, in 750 the Umayyads were overthrown by the Abbasids, who made Baghdad the center of Islamic rule. The circular capital was hailed as "the jewel of the world," and the Abbasids launched the "golden age" of Islam. During their 500-year reign, Omar Khayyam wrote his poetry and Averroes developed his philosophy upon the writings of Aristotle that had been lost to the West. Major advances were made in mathematics and science, including the foundation of algebra and trigonometry forged by Mohammad al-Khawarizmi and Hasan Ibn al-Haitham; the development of modern medicine and the classification of pharmaceuticals by Ibn Sina (Avicenna) and Ali Ibn Rabban at-Tabari; the calculation of the speed of sound, the speed of light, and the circumference of the earth by Abu Raihan al-Biruni; and the formulation of modern chemistry, including the identification of elements and their properties, by Jabir Ibn Haiyan. During the Abbasid caliphate, Muslim cities were the largest in the world, with well-established social services, sewage systems, and paved streets that caused Westerners to marvel.

Because Islam, which had originated as an Arab religion, had come to dominate a vast and culturally diverse population, new questions arose that created a continual need to explain and reinterpret the Koran. Over time, the work of a great number of theologians, jurists, and other scholars produced the Shari'ah, the religio-legal system that came to govern Muslim life. Diversity in the interpretation of the Koran was celebrated, and discourse was the order of the day—until the ninth century, when conservative forces put an end to inquiry and enforced a strictly literal interpretation of the Koran.

In reaction to both the scholarly approach to Islam and the traditionalist revival, the Sufi movement attracted Shi'as and Sunnis who were drawn to the spiritual aspects of Islam. Though there were not a great number of Sufis, by the twelfth century Sufism exercised a strong influence on Muslim theology.

With the arrival of the Mongols in 1258, all of Persia and Iraq were conquered, and a reign of terror ensued the likes of which would not be seen again until barbarism reemerged under Josef Stalin and Adolph Hitler in the twentieth century. Over 16 million Muslims were massacred in Persia and Iraq alone. It took the Mongols 40 days to execute the entire population of Baghdad. Libraries were burned to the ground, cities were razed, and the practice of Islam was outlawed by Mongol law.

Eventually, the Mongols converted to Islam and settled in Muslim lands. Later, Mongol rulers restored mosques, reopened schools, and adopted Muslim culture. They even spread the faith into southern Russia and Eastern Europe. But the power and the glory of the Abbasid dynasty has not been matched since by another Muslim empire.

Nor did the divisions within Islam come to an end. Splinter group grew from splinter group until there were hundreds of sects within the religious bodies. Some were militant; others were pacifistic. Some were socially active; others were ascetically contemplative. Muhammad had predicted such factionalism. He said: "The Jews have broken up into 71 sects. The Christians have broken up into 72 sects. My community will break up into 73, and all of them will be in hellfire except one." When he made his pronouncement, one of his disciples asked, "Which sect will go to Paradise?" The Prophet answered, "The one which I and my companions belong to."

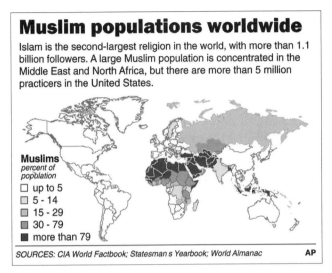

Muslim populations worldwide

Islam is the second-largest religion in the world, with more than 1.1 billion followers. A large Muslim population is concentrated in the Middle East and North Africa, but there are more than 5 million practicers in the United States.

Muslims
percent of population

☐ up to 5
☐ 5 - 14
◻ 15 - 29
◼ 30 - 79
■ more than 79

SOURCES: CIA World Factbook; Statesman s Yearbook; World Almanac   **AP**

(© Associated Press)

The world's major Muslim communities.

Islamic Extremists

Internal conflict and violence have plagued Muslim countries for decades, and the list of Muslim extremist and militant organizations is long. There are many differences between the groups and between the countries they are based in, and it is not within the scope of this book to explore each group in detail. However, there are characteristic variations that will shed some light on the subject at hand: Al Qaeda.

In Islam, politics, ethics, patterns of family life, and daily behavior are inseparable from religious faith and practice. For this reason, every extremist organization is political as well as religious in varying proportions. Some groups have their basis in struggles for social justice in non-Islamic states; others want to overthrow Islamic regimes that have become secularized, though religious piety may not necessarily be the motivation.

PROPERTY OF
NEWBERG HIGH SCHOOL
LIBRARY

Another struggle is an internal one in Islam: the bifurcation of the Sunni and Shi'a Muslims that occurred more than 1,300 years ago. It has been prompting civil wars and widespread persecution in the Islamic world ever since. Islamic extremists and some proportion of moderates of both traditions share many similar goals:

- Opposition to self-serving governments with Western alliances

- Hatred of Israel for its conquest of Jerusalem's Al Aqsa mosque (the third holiest shrine in Islam) and its occupation of Palestine

- Grievances against the Western (colonial) powers, particularly the United States, for ...

    Enabling Israel's occupation of Palestinian lands

    Defiling Islam's holiest shrines, Mecca and Medina, by the presence of its troops in Saudi Arabia

Yet after the attack on America on September 11, 2001, violent fights broke out in the streets of Pakistan between extremist Sunni and extremist Shi'a groups.

Because Al Qaeda members are Sunnis, they stand in opposition to the Shi'a tradition. Radical Sunni beliefs animated the actions of the Taliban, a confederation of Sunni religious leaders. Standing in the Shi'a tradition, in the eyes of Al Qaeda, may not represent apostasy, but it constitutes a serious error that must be corrected.

On April 8, 1998, envoys from Amnesty International reported that thousands of ethnic Hazarahs (Shi'as), mostly men, were killed by the Taliban in the presence of their families. Bin Laden and members of his council were reported to be participants in the killing. The massacre occurred because the Hazarahs refused to compromise their beliefs as Shi'as before the ruling

Taliban. The Hazarahs, who form about 15 percent of Afghanistan's population of 18 million, are part of the Northern Alliance, the group that helped drive the (Sunni) Taliban and Al Qaeda from their strongholds in the Hindu Kush Mountains in December 2001.

But Al Qaeda also stands apart from much of mainstream Sunni Islam, as evidenced by the Muslim nations that have decried the group's acts of terrorism and refused to respond to its call for *jihad.* Is the Islam that Al Qaeda practices and invokes to support its terrorist actions in the true tradition of the Prophet? Osama bin Laden is a Wahhabist (discussed in Chapter 7), a purist Saudi Arabian form of Sunni Islam. Is violence against innocents, then, an aspect of purist Islam?

Some say that bin Laden is battling those he considers enemies of Islam, much as Muhammad battled the Quraish after he went in exile to Medina. Others point to bin Laden's personal history. His Saudi citizenship was revoked because of his extremist activities, which prompts them to wonder if his real agenda is to topple the Saud dynasty and rule a new Islamic empire. The opinions of scholars and analysts aside, Osama bin Laden and his followers quote the Koran at length in Al Qaeda's manual and in all their other statements and assert—as did the Prophet—that only their view of Islam can lead believers to Paradise.

Al Qaeda's position, and the position of other Islamic fundamentalists, purists, and militants, is that the enemy of true belief is not only *outside* the Islamic world, it is within it, that the majority of Muslims in today's society have become *shirks,* or "faithless ones." They stress that Muslims have been humiliated and oppressed by British, Dutch, French, and Russian colonial rule, and by the United States, which supports the interests of repressive Muslim states such as Saudi Arabia. If Muslims return to faith in the infallible teachings of the Koran, they argue, the people of Allah can preserve, restore, and extend their power throughout the world. This is what pious Muslims refer to as the spirit of revivalism.

In *The Observer,* Hazem Saghiyeh, a London-based columnist for the Arabic newspaper *Al Hayat,* was quoted as saying ...

"'Islam—and the Ottoman Empire in particular—was plunged into a deep crisis from which it has never really recovered following the Enlightenment and the Industrial Revolution. For a long time the Muslim world had become isolated and inward-looking and had little contact with the outside world. The new epoch of European supremacy was a trauma and injury to its psyche.' This crisis in the middle of the nineteenth century was accompanied by the emergence of deep divisions in the Islamic world itself over how best to reassert its values. It divided those who argued for reform, modernization and an Islamic Enlightenment from those arguing for Islamic fundamentalism."

—Peter Beaumont, *The Observer,* October 14, 2001

Al Qaeda goes further: In this way, they say, the true believers can convert or subject—by word or by sword—all of mankind to the Shari'ah, the law of Allah that is the underpinning of all of creation. It must be comprehensive in order to be effective. It must involve all Muslims, Sunnis, and Shi'as, and it can come to historical actualization only through the creation of a truly holy Islamic state that allows no transgressions against the teachings of the Koran and the words of the Prophet. Osama bin Laden, along with other Islamic extremists, call this a sacred end that must be achieved by persuasion, guile, or force.

In a January 11, 1999, interview in *Newsweek,* Osama bin Laden said:

> "Hostility toward America is a religious duty, and we hope to be rewarded for it by God. To call us Enemy #1 or #2 does not hurt us. I am confident that Muslims will be able to end the legend of the so-called superpower that is America."

In view of the disaffinity between Al Qaeda's members and Iran's extremists, for example, bin Laden's call for Muslim unity is likely to go unheeded.

4

The Christian Invasion

"In compliance with God's order, we issue the following fatwa to all Muslims: The ruling to kill the Americans and their allies—civilians and military—is an individual duty for every Muslim who can do it in any country in which it is possible to do it, in order to liberate the Al Aqsa Mosque and the holy mosque [Mecca] from their grip, and in order for their armies to move out of all the lands of Islam, defeated and unable to threaten any Muslim. This is in accordance with the words of Almighty God, 'and fight the pagans all together as they fight you all together,' and 'fight them until there is no more tumult or oppression, and there prevail justice and faith in God.'"

—World Islamic Front Statement, *Jihad Against Jews and Crusaders,* February 23, 1998

"Every nation, in every region, now has a decision to make. Either you are with us, or you are with the terrorists."

—President George W. Bush, February 20, 2001

In his declarations of war, Osama bin Laden presents Al Qaeda's jihad not as an armed act of aggression against a foreign power that merits legal deliberation and an imam's pronouncement, but as a defensive struggle against a people who have invaded Muslim lands. This struggle began neither in 1990, when the United States launched Operation Desert Storm, nor in 1947, with the creation of the state of Israel. It began more than 900 years ago in a field in France when a Roman Catholic pope called for a crusade against the Seljuk Turks. It did not take the World Islamic Front's 1998 fatwa to remind the East's Muslims of the Crusades. The first Christian invasion had stayed as fresh in the collective memory as if it had just ended.

Jihad, according to Islamic law, is always permissible to protect believers from foreign aggressors. In such a defensive war, every male Muslim is compelled to participate. Offensive war is a different matter. It can only be justified by certain conditions about which the four schools of Islamic law have conflicting opinions. What's more, offensive war can only be declared by a properly chosen ruler of an Islamic state or by the recognized imam of a religious community.

The Seljuk Turks were not Arabs from a Muslim country, but rather barbarians from the northern steppes of Russia and China who swept over Asia Minor in the eleventh century—much like the Mongol horde of Genghis Khan swept over the same territory two centuries later. They were nomadic warriors who lived off the land, setting up tents wherever they pleased and taking pleasure in sacking cities, pillaging the countryside, and hauling men, women, and children off to slave markets. They were as destructive and unstoppable as a swarm of locusts.

When they conquered Persia, the Seljuk Turks converted to Islam and proceeded to extend their conquests into Christian Byzantium. In August 1071 the Turks confronted the great and mighty army of the Greek Emperor Romanus IV in Armenia, where they defeated the Greek army and carried the emperor off in chains.

Following this great victory, the Turks dispersed in all directions, spreading the fear of God not only among Greek Christians but among the Fatimid (Shi'a) Muslims of Egypt as well. They captured Jerusalem from the Fatimids, seized Antioch from the Greeks, pushed on to Constantinople (today's Istanbul), the great capital of the Byzantine Empire, and toward Cairo, the headquarters of the Fatimid caliph.

In desperation, the Eastern Emperor Alexis Comnena turned to Pope Urban II and the Western princes for military assistance. In a letter, he wrote:

> "I am writing to inform you that the very saintly empire of Greek Christians is daily being persecuted by the Turks. They shamelessly commit the sin of sodomy on our men of all ages and ranks, and, O misery, something that has never been seen or heard of before on our bishops. Already there is nothing for them to conquer except Constantinople, which they threaten to conquer any day now, unless God and the Latin rite come quickly to our aid."

The Emperor went on to appeal to more than their Christian beliefs:

> "The churches of Constantinople are loaded with a vast treasure of gold and silver, gems and precious stones, mantles and cloths of silk, sufficient to decorate all the churches of the world. And, then, too, there are the treasures in the possession of our noble men, not to speak of the treasures of the merchants. No words can describe this wealth of treasure, for it includes not only

the treasuries of the emperors, but also those of the ancient Roman emperors brought here and concealed in the palace. What more can I say? What can be seen by the eye is nothing in comparison with the treasure that remains concealed."

When the pope spoke to the Christian princes that clear, cold day in Clermont, he offered them not only promises of glory and gold, but also an opportunity to obtain eternal salvation. He said:

"Jerusalem implores you to come to its aid. Undertake this journey eagerly for the remission of sins, and be assured of imperishable glory in the Kingdom of Heaven."

The Crusaders

The first crusaders set out in 1098 to rescue the holy tomb of Jesus in Jerusalem from the hands of the Turks. They crushed the Turks in a series of bloody battles in Nicea, Dorylaeum, and Antioch. At the same time, the Fatimids managed to drive the Turks from Jerusalem and send word to the crusaders that the mission had been accomplished and the situation had returned to normal. "We shall restore the Holy City and the Tower of David and Mount Zion to the Christian people," the Fatimid vizier told the Christian princes.

But the crusaders were not content. They were intent upon freeing the Holy Land not just from the Turks but from all Muslims, whom they called Saracens. They now declared war—not simply on an Islamic horde—but on Islam itself.

"For the religious terrorist, violence is first and foremost a sacramental act or divine duty executed in direct response to some theological demand or imperative. Terrorism thus assumes a transcendental dimension, and its perpetrators are consequently unconstrained by the political, moral, or practical constraints that may affect other terrorists."

—Bruce Hoffman, *Inside Terrorism*

On July 14, 1099, the crusaders conquered Jerusalem and put to death more than 70,000 Muslim men, women, and children. They sliced open the bellies of the corpses and extracted their intestines in search of gold coins the Muslims might have swallowed. They then set about to dispose of the bodies, an event recorded as follows by a Frankish chronicler:

> "They also ordered that all the corpses of the Saracens should be thrown outside the city because of the fearful stench; for the whole city was full of their dead bodies. The Saracens who were still alive dragged the dead ones out in front of the gates, and made piles of them, as big as houses. Such a slaughter of pagans no one has seen or heard of; the pyres were like pyramids."

In the wake of the massacre, the Christian armies began to carve out the Crusader States in Palestine and Syria. Thirty years later, Zengi, a charismatic warrior, called upon the Sunni Muslims in Asia Minor to unite against the Christians in a jihad. In 1144, on Christmas Eve, Zengi conquered the Crusader State of Edessa and put the foreign occupiers of the city to death. This momentous event prompted the Second Crusade.

Zengi's son, Nur ed-Din, continued the "holy war" and attempted to unite all Muslims—Sunnis and Shi'as, Arabs and non-Arabs—in the struggle. The division within Islam was so deep that the Fatimid Shi'as opted to unite with the Christian crusaders rather than with their fellow Muslims. Thankfully for the Islamic world, the crusaders, true to their nature, turned on their Muslim allies and spread terror throughout Egypt, killing every man, woman, and child in the city of Bilbeis. They then set out to conquer Cairo. To put an end to such barbarity, the Shi'a Muslims (a.k.a. the Fatimids) of Egypt finally united the Sunni Muslims under Saladin, Nur ed-Din's successor, in a common cause: to drive the Christian armies from Muslim lands.

At the Horn of Hattin in 1187, Saladin, with his great Muslim army, crushed the Christian forces. The bodies of the crusaders were strewn throughout the desert. Imad ed-Din, a Muslim chronicler, was an eyewitness to the carnage:

> "I rode across the battlefield and learned many lessons. I saw heads lying far from bodies, eyes gouged out, bodies covered with powdery ashes, their beauty marred by the claw marks of birds of prey, limbs mangled in battle and scattered about, stumps of flesh, crushed skulls, cloven necks, sliced heads, feet cut off, noses cut off, extremities hacked away, open bellies, shriveled mouths and gaping foreheads out of which eyeballs dangled from sockets."

Saladin then turned his sights on Jerusalem. The attack on the holy city began on September 20, 1187. A Christian defender of the city wrote that the Muslim army came down from the Mount of Olives screaming *"Allahu Akbar"* and blowing trumpets. "Arrows fell like raindrops so that one could not show a finger above the ramparts without being hit. There were so many wounded that all the hospitals and physicians in the city were hard-pressed just to extract missiles from the body."

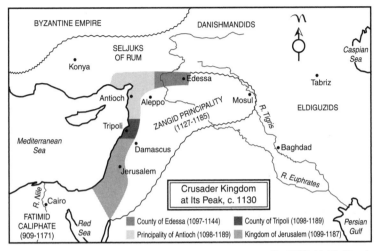

(© AP/Worldwide Photos)

The Crusader Kingdom at its peak in 1130 C.E.

Within two weeks, the Christians surrendered, and Saladin, with his united Muslim army, entered the city in triumph. In sharp contrast to the way the crusaders had conquered Jerusalem 88 years earlier, no booty was taken and not a single resident of the city was harmed.

The fall of Jerusalem gave rise to the third and most glorious crusade, in which the Christian army under Richard the Lion Heart clashed with the mighty forces of Saladin. This great conflict ended in a stalemate, with the Muslims retaining control of Jerusalem.

The last great Christian crusade to free Jerusalem was led by King Louis IX of France, who was canonized as a saint several years after his death. It ended when the Mamelukes, a fierce band of Muslim slave soldiers, completely destroyed not only the Mongol hordes (with whom Louis tried to forge an alliance) but also the Crusader States and every Christian fortress in the Holy

Land. Nevertheless, in the East, the memory of the crusaders' invasion remains at least as strong as that of their kingdom's complete obliteration. For that reason, when on September 13, 2001, President Bush called for a "crusade" against the terrorists who had attacked the Pentagon and the World Trade Center, it was considered a major faux pas, and he has not used the term *crusade* since.

The Ottoman Empire

The Mamelukes ruled Egypt and Syria from 1250 to 1517. Their reign was marked by a continuous series of pogroms and assassinations. They were succeeded by the Ottomans, who arose from the ruins of the rule of the Seljuk Turks. Few historical epochs had a more ironic ending. The Crusades resulted not only in the expansion of Islam, but in the establishment of the Ottoman Turks as the rulers of a vast kingdom, with the old city of Constantinople as its capital.

The Ottoman Empire reached the height of its power under Suleiman the Magnificent (1520–1566). Because of the highly developed firearms of his army (including the first canon), Suleiman's reign extended from Hungary to Yemen and from the Crimea to the Sudan.

After Suleiman's death, it became customary for the male heir to the throne to be raised in the ivory tower of the palace harem, completely removed from the political events and economic conditions of his subjects. As a consequence of this, innocent young sultans with little experience in the ways of the world came to rely on the advice of the grand viziers. Corruption and intrigue abounded. Long and costly wars, including those against the Salavids and the Hapsburgs, sapped the dynasty's military power.

In 1683 the Ottomans failed in an attempt to besiege Vienna. By the terms of the peace treaty with Austria, the Empire lost many of its holdings in Eastern Europe. Things within the Muslim Kingdom went from bad to worse. The economy became stagnant. The eastern Mediterranean and the Red Sea lost much of its economic importance as new trade routes were established between Europe and China. By the end of the nineteenth century, the Ottoman Empire recognized the independence of almost all of the Balkan States and had lost all of North Africa to colonial Europe. The final collapse of the Ottomans' long rule would come with their defeat in World War I and the abolition of the caliphate by Turkish secularists in 1924.

Historians refer to the long span of decline of the Ottoman Empire and the period since then as the "dormition" or "sleeping time" of Islam. Muslim scholars such as Jamaluddin Afghani (1839–1897) and his student Mohammad Abdu sought to reverse the intellectual, political, and cultural slide by attempting to forge a grand synthesis of Islamic religious teachings with Western thought. This philosophic effort was carried over into the twentieth century by such writers and scholars as Syed Abul A'la Maududi, Sayyid Qutb, and Muhammad Iqbal.

But such stirrings could not awaken Islam from its great sleep. That took another shock—the launching of a new invasion from the West against the Prophet's people ...

5

The Jewish Invasion

"Permission to fight is granted to those who are being
persecuted. Since injustice has befallen them, God is
certainly able to support them. They were evicted from
homes unjustly, for no reason other than saying, 'Our
Lord is God.'"
—The Koran (22:39)

The Diaspora of the Jews began with their exile to Babylon in
587 B.C.E. In some countries, they flourished; in others, they
endured persecution and massacre. Those who remained in the
Middle East saw their Second Temple destroyed by the Romans
in 70 C.E., but for much of the period of Muslim rule, they,
along with the Christians and other non-Muslims, enjoyed the
relative safety granted to protected minorities. Under the crusaders, and the Mongols and Mamelukes who followed, Jews
were subject to the same brutalities as the Muslims: They were
massacred, raped, robbed, and sold into slavery.

The Diasporan Jews continued to suffer persecution in
many parts of the world. In the nineteenth century, the regular-
ity and severity of the pogroms in Russia began to drive them
back to the Holy Land; by 1845, the Jewish community was the
largest one in Jerusalem.

The Jewish "invasion" of Palestine began with a dream of a new Zion, the dream of Theodore Herzl (1860–1904), a Viennese journalist who believed that Jews could not escape anti-Semitism through assimilation in any country. The only place where Jews could be safe from persecution, Herzl thought, would be a Jewish sovereign state—the *Judenstaadt*. The most logical place to establish this state, he believed, would be Palestine, the ancient Jewish homeland.

> "Those Jews who rely on the biblical deed to the land take their history from the ancient period of four thousand years or so ago, skipping easily over the centuries of Muslim rule that followed; those Arabs who regard history as their ally tend to begin with the Muslim conquests in the seventh century C.E., blithely ignoring the Jewish kingdoms that existed here two thousand years before Muhammad made his appearance."
> —David K. Shipler, from *Arab and Jew*

Herzl formed the World Zionist Organization with the purpose of "the establishment of a home for the Jewish people secured under public law in Palestine." The organization gained widespread support. Between 1880 and 1890, more than 20,000 European Jews settled in Palestine as the first *aliyah* ("going up") for the creation of the Judenstaadt.

Aliyah

The second aliyah took place between 1900 and 1914 and brought 40,000 more Jewish immigrants to the Holy Land. Many of the newcomers who belonged to socialist Zionist organizations became farmers and formed communal agricultural settlements (*kibbutzim*).

The third aliyah began in 1915. Two years later Arthur James Lord Balfour expressed the British government's commitment to the creation of "a national home for the Jewish people." It became known as the Balfour Declaration.

> Foreign Office
> November 2, 1917
>
> Dear Lord Rothschild,
>
> I have much pleasure in conveying to you, on behalf of His Majesty's Government, the following declaration of sympathy with Jewish Zionist aspirations which has been submitted to, and approved by, the Cabinet.
>
> "His Majesty's Government view with favour the establishment in Palestine of a national home for the Jewish people, and will use their best endeavours to facilitate the achievement of this object, it being clearly understood that nothing shall be done which may prejudice the civil and religious rights of existing non-Jewish communities in Palestine, or the rights and political status enjoyed by Jews in any other country."
>
> I should be grateful if you would bring this declaration to the knowledge of the Zionist Federation.
>
> Yours sincerely,
> Arthur James Balfour

All of this was taking place against the backdrop of the dismantling of the Ottoman Empire (1453–1923), which would create a new map of the Near East. In 1919 the Treaty of Versailles provided for the provisional independence of Arab countries formerly under Ottoman rule. This was a time of great intrigue: T. E. Lawrence (Lawrence of Arabia) was leading an Arab uprising against the Turks while the British and French played the "great game"—carving up the Near East to secure their future interests in the region. The competing agendas of the Arab leaders, and of Britain and France, dragged on through a series of complicated negotiations until, in 1922, the League of Nations acted. France was mandated with the responsibility for Syria and Lebanon. Iraq and Palestine would be under the British mandate.

Another 40,000 Jewish immigrants had arrived in Palestine by the end of the third aliyah in 1925. That same year, a record 34,000 Jews arrived, and the Jewish population more than doubled. It had reached 160,000.

Even though the Balfour Declaration protected the rights of non-Jewish communities in Palestine, Palestinians did not take too kindly to it, or to the influx of Jewish settlers. The Jews drove the Arab *fellaheen* (peasant farmers) from their land and into squalid settlements. Palestine resistance movements sprung up, and protests erupted. In 1927 a riot took place in Hebron in which 135 Jews were killed and 350 wounded.

To protect the settlers, the Jews formed military organizations such as the *Haganah* to squelch any disturbances among the displaced Palestinians.

During the fourth aliyah, which lasted from 1925 to the start of World War II, the number of *Yishuv* (Jews in Palestine) increased to 500,000. The Jews now represented more than 30 percent of the population of Palestine, and their holdings more than doubled, from 150,000 acres to 382,250. With their savings, the Jews were able to purchase more and more land from wealthy Arab landowners, forcing more and more Palestinians to pack up their belongings and move to settlements. More riots erupted. More Jews were killed.

Terrorism Takes Hold

In 1928 the Muslim Brotherhood, a group of Islamic purists, sprung up in Egypt for the purpose of upholding the tenets of Islam in a modernizing society. They later aided in the Palestinian cause. In 1938 the British drew up a partition plan for the creation of two separate states, and in a move to appease the Arabs, the British governors of Palestine began to restrict Jewish immigration. As a result, the number of new arrivals fell from 66,000 in 1935 to 14,000 in 1938. But the Arabs were not pacified. The riots and attacks continued, killing more than 300 Jews and wounding 600 within a 6-month period.

Palestine under the British mandate, 1923 to 1948, and the British partition plan.

The Jews turned to terrorism. The Irgun (the National Military Organization) fought both the Arabs and the British. All hell began to break loose. The Irgun bombed government offices, police departments, and the King David Hotel in Jerusalem. They attacked trains, assassinated the British minister of state, and stormed the British prison at Acre.

Meanwhile, Nazi Germany had begun the "final solution" to the Jewish Question. Many of those who managed to escape found their way to Palestine. By the end of World War II, six million Jews had been put to death by the Nazis. The world's compassion for the Jews was at an all-time high as Holocaust survivors poured into Palestine. The Arab population was at the breaking point. It was impossible for Britain to act on their behalf. Jewish militants were attacking their officials and installations throughout Palestine. In 1947 the British threw up their hands and turned the situation over to the United Nations.

The UN General Assembly came up with a partition plan that called for the division of Palestine into two states: one for Jews, one for Arabs. This solution seemed acceptable to the Jews, but the Arab Higher Committee called upon Arabs to "fight for every inch of their country." By this time, the Jewish population had reached 650,000. Violence erupted throughout the country, including a bloody massacre of Arabs that took place at Deir Yassin.

The United Nations replaced Britain's Palestine partition plan with one more favorable to the Zionists. The neighboring Arab states now rallied to the Palestinian cause. The British stated that they would leave the troubled country on May 14, 1948.

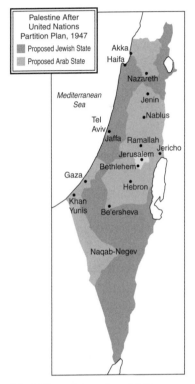

The UN partition plan, 1947.

On May 14, 1948, Israel—the Judenstaadt of Herzl—declared its independence as a nation. The next day, five Arab armies from Egypt, Syria, Transjordan, Lebanon, and Iraq invaded the new Jewish state. Israel was quickly able to repel the attack and occupy most of the Palestinian lands, but the cost to the new nation was enormous. A total of 6,373 Israelis were killed, nearly 1 percent of the population, and Israel's military expenditures were in excess of $500 million.

Palestine after Israeli occupation, 1949.

In the wake of the war, more than 200,000 Palestinians left their homeland; some left of their own accord, others were driven from towns and villages by Israeli soldiers. The problem became so acute that the United States established a relief fund for Palestinian refugees with a budget of $50 million.

By this time, French troops had left Syria and Lebanon, Jordan had become an independent kingdom, and Saudi Arabia had emerged from World War II a fabulously oil-rich monarchy.

The British and French empires had begun to disintegrate, and the post-Ottoman world was struggling to achieve some degree of stability.

Newly independent Arab states were continually changing the map of the Middle East and North Africa, but nationhood was still an unfamiliar idea. Repeated attempts at creating Arab unity floundered, as Egypt, the largest and most established Arab country, maintained a discreet distance from the fray. The vacuum that had been left by the end of almost 500 years of Ottoman rule was followed by the departure of the British and French from the Middle East and North Africa—Islam was beginning to take hold as a unifying force. American oil interests had produced enormous wealth for the ruling class of Saudi Arabia and the Gulf states. The State of Israel, surrounded by countries that desired its destruction, had the unequivocal support and protection of the U.S. government. Inevitably, the nascent Muslim states that found themselves in political and economic chaos responded to the appeal of socialism. And in the Soviet Union, they found a powerful, anti-capitalist, anti-American ally.

The Six Day War

In June 1967, Egyptian president Gamal Nasser blockaded Israel's access to the Gulf of Aqaba on the Egypt-Israel border. Israel's response was instantaneous and stunning: In six days, it destroyed Egypt's air force and pushed back the armies of Syria, Jordan, and Lebanon. When it was all over, Israel occupied the West Bank, the Gaza Strip, the Sinai Peninsula, East Jerusalem, and the Golan Heights. The humiliating defeat had a major impact on the growth and intensity of militant Islamic movements. Al Qaeda leader Ayman al-Zawahiri, in an excerpt from

Knights Under the Banner of the Prophet, published in *The New York Times* (December 9, 2001) expressed it this way:

> "The most important event that influenced the jihad movement in Egypt was 'the Setback' of 1967. The symbol, Gamal Abdel Nasser, fell. His followers tried to portray him to the people as if he was the eternal leader who could never be conquered. The tyrant leader who used to threaten and pledge in his speeches to wipe out his enemies turned into a winded man chasing a peaceful solution to save at least a little face."

Territories annexed by Israel following Six Day War, 1967.

Yasir Arafat's Palestine Liberation Organization (PLO), and Fatah, its military wing, went into high gear, agitating for Palestinian rule in Jordan and Israel. Their expulsion from Jordan in 1970 drove them to Lebanon, a morass of complicated alliances that became the battleground for Syria, Israel, and Palestinian militant groups. In addition to the PLO, Hamas, Islamic Jihad, and others, Hizballah, an organization of militant Shi'as supported by Iran, committed itself to taking whatever actions necessary to drive Israeli troops out of Southern Lebanon. Some scholars say that it was at that time that the Palestinian occupation began to become not just an Arab cause, but a Muslim cause as well.

When Israeli troops entered Lebanon in 1978 to weed out the bases used by the PLO to launch terrorist attacks on Israel, Beirut was in the middle of a full-scale factional war. In the years that followed, much of the country was destroyed by internal as well as external conflict. An agreement for Israeli withdrawal from Lebanon was finally negotiated in 1984, and the United States sent troops to Beirut to secure the airport so that Israeli troops could leave peacefully. A Muslim Druze sect was making serious threats against the safety of the U.S. Marines, so President Reagan sent a flotilla of Navy warships to the Lebanese coast. Muslim extremists saw this as an act of aggression by the United States–Israel alliance. It prompted a Muslim suicide bomber to blow up the Marine barracks in Beirut, killing 241 personnel.

When Saddam Hussein invaded Kuwait in 1990 to force the emirate to lower oil production, the United States launched a missile attack on Baghdad. By the end of the conflict that became known as Desert Storm, 370 Allied troops were killed (most by friendly fire), but the death toll for Iraqis exceeded 35,000 civilians. Osama bin Laden later would compare the bombing of Iraq to the American bombing of Nagasaki at the close of World War II.

"My Muslim Brothers of the World:

"Your brothers in Palestine and in the land of the two Holy Places are calling upon your help and asking you to take part in fighting against the enemy—your enemy and their enemy—the Americans and the Israelis. They are asking you to do whatever you can, with your own means and ability, to expel the enemy, humiliated and defeated, out of the sanctities of Islam ...."

—Excerpt from fatwa issued by Osama bin Laden, August 23, 1996

President Clinton sent more U.S. troops abroad than any president had since 1945, most of them to Muslim countries. Under a UN mission called Operation Restore Hope, Clinton sent troops to Somalia to end the rivalry between hundreds of diverse clans, all of them Muslim. Troops were sent to Bosnia as part of the NATO peacekeeping force. Clinton bombed Iraq, Afghanistan, Sudan, and Serbia. A group of Islamic terrorists decided to retaliate and bomb the Pentagon and the financial capital of the "great aggressor." In Jerusalem, the navel of monotheism, there are more Jews and Palestinians being killed every day.

6

Formula for Terror

"The leadership of western man in the human world is coming to an end .... The turn of Islam has come."
—Sayyid Qutb, *Signposts on the Path*

"Jihad and the rifle alone: no negotiations, no conferences and no dialogues."
—Abdullah Azzam, *Nida'ul Islam,* July 1996

The religious ideological ancestry of Al Qaeda can be traced to Wahhabism, a purist Sunni Islamic movement that developed in Arabia at the time of the American Revolution. Muhammad ibn Abdul Wahhab (1703–1791), the founder of the movement, sought to bring about a spiritual revolution through the purging of moral and spiritual innovations that had accumulated since the time of Muhammad.

Abdul Wahhab was born into a wealthy and scholarly family from the central Arabian area of Najd. He began speaking to various Bedouin tribes about the need for Muslims to return to the "golden age" of Islam that existed at the advent of the Abbasid dynasty in 750—the age when the Muslims were the masters of all they surveyed, and the rulers of the West were Goths, Berbers, Egyptians, Greeks, Syrians, Chaldeans, Persians, and Kurds.

In order to achieve this return, Abdul Wahhab instructed his followers to live by an uncompromising interpretation of the Koran and to uphold the following prohibitions:

- No other object for worship than Allah
- No use of prayer beads
- No other name in prayer except Allah
- No smoking of tobacco
- No abusive language
- No ornamentation in mosques, including minarets

Calling themselves *mawahhidun* (confessors of unity) this sect became a formidable force when Abdul Wahhab converted Ibn Saud, the leader of the largest Bedouin tribe in the Arabian Peninsula, and instructed Saud's tribesmen in the tenets of true belief—and in the use of firearms.

The Wahhabists conquered much of the Arabian Peninsula and, by the end of the eighteenth century, had amassed enough power to challenge the Ottoman Empire on the borders of the Fertile Crescent. They were eventually defeated by the Ottoman army and forced to return to the desert. But the movement never died. It received new impetus in 1947 when the UN mandate called for the creation of a Jewish Palestinian state and, it followed, the creation of the Arab suicide squads (*fedayeen*) to terrorize Jews and drive them from the Palestinian homeland.

In 1929 Hassan al-Banna, an Egyptian schoolteacher, formed an organization called the Society of the Muslim Brotherhood. The Society emerged against the background of growing resentment against foreign domination of Arab lands. It stood in opposition to the Islamic Reformation, a progressive organization that sought to reinterpret the traditional teachings of Islam in hopes of delivering Muslim countries from their backwardness and "lack of enlightenment." This, for al-Banna, represented heresy and an abandonment of the revealed truths of the Islamic faith. He envisioned—in the spirit of the Wahhabists—a return to the original form and spirit of Islam.

The Muslim Brotherhood

The Muslim Brotherhood had a dual purpose. One purpose was to proclaim the uncompromising moral and spiritual teachings of the Koran in order to bring about a revival; the other was to acquire arms and to forge a guerilla army for the creation of a pan-Islamic state. In 1948 members of the Brotherhood fought against the Zionists in Palestine and staged a series of violent protests against the Egyptian government. They assassinated judges, and in 1949, struck down the prime minister. Two months later, al-Banna was murdered as an act of retaliation against his group. The Brotherhood hovered on the fringes of legality until Egyptian president Gamal Nasser, who had survived one of the Brotherhood's assassination attempts, outlawed the group and freed many of its members to flee to other countries. The Brotherhood managed to survive and even flourish. In 1982 it led an uprising of Syrian Sunni Muslims that was crushed by Syrian leader Hafez Assad.

An influential member of the Muslim Brotherhood was Sayyid Qutb, the so-called "father of modern Islamic fundamentalism." In his most influential work, *Signposts on the Road,* Qutb maintained that all Christians and Jews are destined for hell. But his fiercest polemics were directed against Muslims who did not abide by the teachings of the faith (apostates), such as President Nasser of Egypt and King Saud of Saudi Arabia. These corrupt regimes, Qutb said, had to be resisted and overthrown.

The Office of Services

In 1979, the year Soviet troops invaded Afghanistan, Abdullah Azzam, a Palestinian member of the Brotherhood, established a recruiting office called *Maktab al-Khidamat* (the Office of Services) to recruit young Muslims for the Afghan front. This office, in time, would be transformed into the terrorist group known as Al Qaeda (the Base).

One of the young recruits was a Saudi millionaire, Osama bin Laden, a Wahhabist. Bin Laden was enthusiastic about the war effort and agreed to fund the establishment of branches of the Office of Services throughout the world, Europe and the United States included.

Another recruit was an Algerian scholar, Abdullah Anas. Anas recalled his first encounter with bin Laden to Stephen Engelberg in a January 14, 2001, *New York Times* article:

> "He was one of the guys who came to the jihad in Afghanistan. But, unlike the others, what he had was a lot of money. He's not very sophisticated politically and organizationally. But he's an activist with a great imagination. He ate very little. He slept very little. Very generous. He'd give you his clothes."

When bin Laden returned from the front, he would stay with Azzam and the new recruits and sleep on the floor. "You see," Azzam would like to tell the volunteers, "this man has everything in his own country. You see, he lives with all the poor people in this room." The two became fast friends. Azzam traveled throughout the Middle East, the United Kingdom, and the United States to raise money and recruits for the Afghan cause, while bin Laden provided financial support, handled military matters, and brought to Afghanistan from around the world experts in guerrilla warfare, sabotage, and covert operations.

Within a year, thousands of volunteers were training in bin Laden's boot camp in Peshawar. Most (more than 5,000) came from bin Laden's native Saudi Arabia. Others came from Algeria (3,000), Egypt (2,000) and thousands more came from other Muslim countries such as Yemen, Pakistan, and Sudan. A major function of the Office of Services was to prevent outbursts of violence between the Sunni and the Shi'a volunteers and to keep the focus of the recruits on the jihad and the teachings of the Koran.

The Soviet-Afghan war set the stage for the last stand-off between the Soviet Union and the United States. The Americans, at that time, had the same goals as the *Mujahedeen* of bin Laden and Azzam—the defeat of the Soviets. To weigh the balance in favor of the Afghans, the CIA launched a $500 million-a-year effort to arm and train the impoverished and outgunned guerilla army. The most promising guerilla leaders were singled out for sophisticated training in advanced weaponry. They were still in Afghanistan in 2001 when the United States launched its attack on Al Qaeda and Taliban strongholds.

Egypt's Islamic Jihad

Toward the end of the war, a group from the Egyptian Islamic Jihad arrived in Peshawar for a special meeting with bin Laden and Azzam. One of the Egyptians was Ayman al-Zawahiri, a physician from Cairo and the former leader of the Egyptian Islamic Jihad, the group that assassinated Egyptian president Anwar Sadat. Another was Sheikh Omar Abd al-Rahman, a radical religious scholar. They courted bin Laden, hoping to secure his financial support for their pet projects, including the assassinations of President Muhammad Zia ul-Haq of Pakistan and President Hosni Mubarak of Egypt, who, in their opinion, had become apostates.

Bin Laden was taken with al-Zawahiri, who he called "the Doctor" because of his education, erudition, and commitment to jihad against the Soviets, the Jews, and the United States. The Doctor first arrived in Afghanistan in 1980 to take part in the war effort. With his poor vision and lack of military training, he proved to be of little use in combat, but he was extremely valuable in providing medical care and treatment for the troops. He was also skillful in attracting new recruits and soliciting financial support. For these purposes, al-Zawahiri traveled back and forth from Afghanistan to Egypt.

As an expression of his friendship, the Doctor "loaned" two of his men to bin Laden; they would become lynchpins of Al Qaeda: Muhammad Atef and Abu Ubayda al-Banshiri. Atef became Al Qaeda's operational planner. He was killed in a U.S. air strike on Afghanistan in November 2001. Abu Ubaydah al-Banshiri served as second in command of the Al Qaeda military. He later drowned in a ferry accident on Lake Victoria.

Bin Laden gradually drifted away from his old friend Azzam and toward his new Egyptian associates. As the gap between their visions of the future widened, the lively dialogue that had characterized their friendship declined into bitter argument. One night, Azzam confided to Anas: "I'm very worried about Osama. This heaven-sent man, like an angel. I am worried about his future if he stays with these people."

The Office of Services meetings were now a battleground. Azzam argued that the group should concentrate its efforts on the creation of an Islamic state in Afghanistan that, in time, could gain the support of Muslims throughout the Middle East and, in time, wage war against Israel. The Egyptians disagreed, and so did bin Laden, saying that such a war should be fought against several of the *kafir* (infidel) countries simultaneously.

Azzam saw little difference between the United States and the Soviet Union, contending that they were both hostile to Islam. But he opposed terrorism against the United States, because it would involve military action against a nation that does not border an Islamic state. The Egyptians disagreed. So did bin Laden.

Soon Azzam found himself on the outs with bin Laden and the Egyptians, who began to plot tactics for the continuation of the jihad in private. Azzam no longer had a say in the operations of the Office of Services.

In 1986, according to Middle Eastern intelligence services, bin Laden established his own training camp for Persian Gulf Arabs, a group of about 50 commandos who lived in tents apart from the Afghan fighters. He called his new camp *Al Masahah,* "the lion's den."

The Formation of Al Qaeda

In 1988, a year before the Soviet withdrawal from Afghanistan, bin Laden and the Egyptian terrorists formed Al Qaeda. They began to move ahead with their plans. They funneled huge sums into creating the infrastructure of what was to serve as the base for their jihad against the apostate Muslim governments, Israel, and the United States. They represented a small band of believers, but they had the potential to accomplish their mission. They had received training in sophisticated weapons. They had an arsenal of high-tech weapons, including Stinger antiaircraft missiles. They had financial resources through bin Laden's personal fortune, contributions to charitable organizations, and the lucrative drug trade in Afghanistan, with laboratories to refine heroin. The ruling Taliban, enforcers of the most extreme and repressive form of fundamentalist Islam, became Al Qaeda's private militia.

Al Qaeda became, in effect, the shadow government of a sovereign state. The madrasahs turned out students steeped in the teachings of Islam and hatred of the West. The training camps transformed those chosen to fight the jihad into skilled and disciplined terrorists.

An office that had been used to support the Afghan war effort had become a highly financed and structured terrorist organization.

The Mujahedeen were wildly successful. In 10 years of fighting, they managed to bring about the defeat of the Soviet invaders and contribute to the collapse of the Soviet Union. The CIA, by arming and training the Muslim guerillas, had achieved their objective. The Reagan administration won a great victory. The defeated Soviet troops left behind a huge arsenal of sophisticated weapons and thousands of seasoned and highly trained Islamic warriors.

Shortly after the war ended, Azzam and his two sons were killed by a car bomb in Peshawar as they drove to a mosque for Friday prayer services.

The murders were never solved.

Growth of "the Base"

The men who had been recruited by the Office of Services for the jihad returned to their countries, trained in establishing terrorist cells that could turn to "the Base" for a steady supply of money, weapons, manpower, and terrorist training.

In Jordan, Al Qaeda's Mujahedeen veterans created the Jaysh-e-Mohammed with the aim of toppling the government of King Hussein. In their eyes, Hussein, whose family claimed descent from the Prophet Muhammad, with his Western style and American wife, represented an impious affront to Islamic fundamentalism.

In Algeria, another group with links to the Base, the Armed Islamic Group (known by the French initials GIA) blew up military targets and slaughtered hundreds of Algerians who opposed the holy war.

In Egypt, Al-Gama'a al-Islamiyya set about planning to assassinate Egyptian president Hosni Mubarak.

Other terrorist groups and organizations popped up throughout the world. Among those that had varying levels and degrees of links to Al Qaeda were the following:

- The Jihad Organization of Jordan
- The Pakistani Al-Hadith Group
- The Lebanese Partisans League
- The Bayt al-Imam Group of Jordan
- Asbat al-Ansar (Lebanon)
- Harakat al-Ansar/Mujahadeen (Pakistan)
- Al-Badar (Pakistan)
- Talaa al Fath (Vanguards of Conscience)
- The Groupe Roubaix (Canada/France)
- Harakat ul Jihad (Pakistan)
- Jaysh-e-Mohammed (Pakistan)
- Jamiat Ulema-e-Islam (JUI/Pakistan)
- Hizballah (Lebanon)
- Hezb ul-Mujahideen (Pakistan)
- Islamic Movement of Uzbekistan
- The Jihad Group of Bangladesh
- The Jihad Group of Yemen

- Lashkar-e-Tayyiba (Pakistan)
- Lebanese Partisans Group
- Moro Islamic Liberation Front (Philippines)
- The Partisans Movement (Kashmir)
- Abu Sayyaf (Philippines)
- Al-Ittihad (Somalia)
- Ulema Union of Afghanistan
- Takfir wal Hijra (Algeria, Egypt)

The goals of Al Qaeda and its terrorist branches were straight-forward:

- To radicalize existing Islamic groups throughout the world
- To overthrow all Muslim governments that had become apostate
- To support Muslim fighters in Afghanistan, Algeria, Bosnia, Chechnya, Eritrea, Kosovo, Pakistan, Somalia, Tajikistan, and Yemen
- The destruction of the State of Israel
- The destruction of the United States of America
- The abolition of all national borders between Islamic states
- The union of all Muslims in the creation of an international Muslim government "that follows the rules of the caliph"

The Base was organized unlike any other terrorist organization. It consisted of hundreds of cells that operated independently of one another and yet in tandem with the objectives of the organization. It was a hydra. If you cut off one head, another would appear, and another, and another. It was designed to ensure that no nation, not even the United States of America, would be able to kill it. In its global reach and unfathomable structure, it was unlike any force that had ever been unleashed against the United States or any other nation.

Following the war, bin Laden returned to Saudi Arabia, where he organized a branch of Al Qaeda whose aim it was to eliminate the presence of U.S. military forces in the homeland of the Prophet and the two most sacred cities in the world: Mecca and Medina. Realizing that there was a jackal in their midst, Saudi officials sought the arrest of bin Laden. He fled to Sudan, where a group of Islamic extremists had taken control of the government, and where he was greeted with open arms.

Bin Laden in Sudan

In Sudan bin Laden established three camps in the north to train young Muslims in the tenets of Islam and the techniques of terrorism, and two farms in the south to provide shelter to fugitive terrorists.

As soon as he got settled in Khartoum, he met with Egyptians members of Al Qaeda, including Ramzi Ahmed Yousef, to plan the bombing of the World Trade Center in New York City. Suicide bombers were recruited from Egypt and Saudi Arabia, and the first attack on America got underway. It was a spectacular success. The car bomb rocked the World Trade Center on February 26, 1993, killing six and injuring more than a thousand. The damage was in excess of $500 million. Bin Laden was elated, and special prayer services of thanksgiving were held in his apartment.

Several weeks after the bombing, bin Laden paid to transfer more than 500 Mujahedeen veterans to Sudan to train for the next battle of the jihad. At that time, his overriding desire was to drive the U.S. forces from Somalia where they were engaged in a peacekeeping mission called Operation Restore Hope. The primary purpose of the mission was to deliver food to the starving Muslim people and to protect them from the local warlords. Bin Laden issued fatwas for an attack on all American soldiers and civilians in Saudi Arabia, Yemen, and the Horn of Africa.

In 1993 bin Laden opened a key cell in Kenya as a "gateway to Somalia." Members of Al Qaeda blended into the local population by opening a series of "legitimate" businesses: One bought and sold diamonds, another sold fish, and a third operated as an Islamic charity for victims of American aggression.

On October 3, 1993, a force highly trained by Al Qaeda crossed over into Somalia and ambushed a unit of the U.S. peacekeeping force. In the wake of the attack, 18 Americans and several hundred Somalis were left dead. Osama bin Laden and other Al Qaeda members were indicted in 1998 by the United States for training the perpetrators.

Overnight, other Islamic terrorist cells sprouted up throughout Africa, including key cells in Kenya and Nairobi that prepared for additional attacks on American troops.

During that period, the mild-mannered bin Laden had remained in his small apartment in Khartoum with his four wives and his children. He opened a new Islamic bank, a tannery, a transportation company, and a construction firm. He openly expressed his admiration for Sudan, and he especially liked its leader, Dr. Hassan Abdullah al-Turabi, a graduate of the Sorbonne and the former head of the Muslim Brotherhood. In 1983 al-Turabi had declared that the country would be governed by a strict interpretation of the *Shari'ah,* or the laws of Islam.

Bin Laden found other things to like about Sudan, including the slave trade. He began purchasing small children to pick marijuana on his farms in the Nile River valley just north of Khartoum. He also put the slave children to work on his large sunflower plantation. The price for such slaves was most reasonable. He could purchase a healthy young boy or girl of eight or nine who had been snatched from Uganda for one AK-47. Such a weapon could be bought in Darra, a munitions market outside Peshawar, Pakistan, for less than $200. One slave trader complained that he once had been cheated by bin Laden, who gave him 98 guns for 100 children. The slave trade is alive and well in Sudan. Since 1995 more than 11,000 slaves have been freed in the country by the Swiss-based group Christian Solidarity. The UN Children's Fund says that the practice of buying slaves and releasing them only serves to increase the trade.

But bin Laden's heart remained with the jihad and the task of driving kafirs (infidels) from the holy land of the Prophet. He instituted a policy of blackmail and terror that extended from Sudan into Egypt and Libya. Non-Muslim businessmen were forced to pay a required tax for the jihad and to act in the unassuming manner of *dhimmis* (non-Muslims living in Muslim states) before their Muslim superiors—a practice that had begun in the Medina of Muhammad's time. Those who refused to pay found their businesses in ashes and their lives in danger. The program became so successful that insurance companies refused to grant policies to non-Muslim businesses.

At the instigation of Al Qaeda, Christians were slaughtered throughout Sudan and in other areas of Africa and the Near East. In the Nuba Mountain region, Amnesty International workers found the bodies of hundreds of decapitated Christians whose hands and feet had been severed from their bodies by members of the National Islamic Front, a terrorist group that was funded, supported, and manned by Al Qaeda members. The Amnesty workers further discovered that hundreds of women and children had been rounded up and sold as slaves from Al Qaeda's Nsitu camp, 15 miles from Juba in southern Sudan.

In a recent interview, Jamar Al Fafa, a member of the National Islamic Front, boasted of attacking Christian settlements throughout Sudan with "Afghan Arabs." "Yes," he told me, "I served the emir [bin Laden]." He went on …

> "The Afghan veterans were very pious men. All were obedient to Allah and his Prophet (Allah's blessings and salutations on him). In the north, people were living as Christians and never heard of the true faith. Some were killed, but not very many. It sometimes happens in such circumstances. We had to teach them to pray in a proper way by facing the birthplace of the Prophet (Allah's greetings and salutations on him). We told them to never spit or defecate in that direction. We told them to eat clean food and not unclean pig meat. Many were unclean—physically and spiritually. The men were not circumcised as Abraham instructed. Some refused to bear the mark of redemption. They were not real converts, only play actors. Any real convert will openly submit to the will of Allah. To be a believer means to submit. And so we set about to circumcise them. Many knew how to remove the foreskin cleanly so that there was very little bleeding. We also circumcised the kafir women who were extended almost like small boys."

According to Christian news services, more than two million people died or were put to death in Sudan during the 1990s as a result of famine, sanctioned genocide, and military action by the government and terrorist groups. Millions of Sudanese lost their homes and possessions as thousands of villages were put to flame in the name of the holy war.

In a trip to southern Sudan in 1998, Britain's Baroness Caroline Cox uncovered widespread destruction and loss of life. Vast areas of the Bahr-El-Ghazal were laid waste by the National Islamic Front at the command of bin Laden's Afghan Arabs and the government-sponsored Mujahedeen. More than 160 bodies were found and hundreds were reported missing. Lady Caroline said that countless bodies could be seen floating in a river.

In the midst of this havoc, bin Laden began his quest for nuclear weapons. This information was confirmed by the testimony of Jamal Ahmed al-Fadl, a Sudanese national, who was the U.S. government's "Confidential Source Number One" on the operations of Al Qaeda.

On behalf of bin Laden, al-Fadl made arrangements for the purchase of uranium from former Sudanese officials who represented businessmen from South Africa. The uranium, he said, was contained in a three-foot-high cylinder that bore a serial number and the English words, "South Africa." Uranium is the element required to extract plutonium, the primary ingredient of a nuclear weapon. The arranged price for the cylinder was $1.5 million. Bin Laden was delighted with the deal, paid the money, and had the uranium tested in the town of Hilat Koko in Cyprus.

Al Qaeda was becoming dangerous—more dangerous than most Middle Eastern nations. It was in the process of obtaining weapons of mass destruction.

Terrorist Attacks

Bin Laden's interlude in Sudan was coming to an end. In his years in the desert, he and his group had accomplished a great deal:

- The bombing of the World Trade Center in New York, which had killed 6 and injured 1,042

- The attack on the U.S. peacekeeping forces in Somalia

- The bombing of a hotel in Yemen, a favorite watering hole for kafirs and apostates, in December 1992

- The creation of terrorist cells throughout North and South Africa to train hundreds of soldiers for the jihad

- The religious cleansing of Christians and other kafirs throughout the Sudan

- The financing of the Gulf Battalion of the Iranian Guardians of the Revolution, headed by the Yemeni fundamentalist 'Abd al-Mayid al-Zandani, for deployment to countries throughout the Persian Gulf when circumstances permitted

- A car bombing of the Egyptian Embassy in Islamabad, Pakistan, which killed more than 20 Egyptians and Pakistanis, carried out by the Egyptian Islamic Jihad, a key component of Al Qaeda

- The widespread political upheavals throughout the Middle East and North Africa, including those in Pakistan and Algeria; the Algerian jihad warriors had managed to sack a government building and seize thousands of blank passports that would permit members of

Al Qaeda to change identities and travel anywhere in the world

- The first step into the Atomic Age—obtaining the means to create a nuclear warhead

Naturally, there had been disappointments, such as several failed attempts to blow up U.S. airliners in the Pacific, the botched assassination of Pope John Paul II (who previously had survived an assassination attempt by a member of the Muslim Brotherhood), and last but not least, the poorly conceived plot to murder Egyptian president Mubarak in Ethiopia in June 1995. But these disappointments were minor in the vast scheme of the times.

constitution. The flag bore the sword of Islam and the Shahadah (the Islamic confession of faith): "I bear witness that there is no god but Allah and Muhammad is his prophet."

"King Abdel Aziz unified the Arabian Peninsula some 70 years ago through a pact with adherents of the austere Wahhabi sect who made a return to simplicity their trademark. His descendants have long sought to wrap themselves tightly in that legacy. They know Saudi Arabia enjoys unparalleled prestige among the world's one billion Muslims as the land where the Prophet Muhammad and the faith were born, the land that uses the Koran for its Constitution, and every year welcomes millions of Muslims on the hajj, or pilgrimage to the holiest shrines of Mecca and Medina … meanwhile extremists chip away at the foundations of al-Saud control."
—Neil MacFarquhar, *The New York Times*, September 6, 2001

Osama bin Laden, himself a Wahhabist, condemns Saudi king Fahd above all others for his hypocritical public support of purist Wahhabism while the king himself corrupts its principles by living impiously and consorting with the United States.

Bin Laden in Saudi Arabia

Bin Laden was born the seventeenth son of 51 children of Muhammad bin Laden. His father was of Yemeni descent from the village of Al-Ribat; his mother was a Saudi. Muhammad bin Laden left Al-Ribat in 1931 and established a construction company in Saudi Arabia with his brothers. The company obtained enormous government contracts and built everything from mosques in Mecca and Medina to highways and palaces. By the time Osama was born, the company already was worth more than $2 billion.

(© AP/Worldwide Photos)

Osama bin Laden and his son, at his son's wedding, 2001.

Osama was raised in a household of devout Wahhabists, and he, like his brothers and sisters, was educated in Wahhabist schools. The Saudis who serve as the leaders of Al Qaeda are also Wahhabists. This accounts for the FBI finding that the major source of financial support for bin Laden and the terrorists comes not from Pakistan but from Saudi Arabia, would-be ally of the United States in the war against terrorism. Some of this support is allegedly solicited by a Saudi organization called The Muslim World League. On its website, The Muslim World League proclaims its goal of repelling "inimical trends and dogmas which the enemies of Islam seek to exploit in order to destroy the unity of Muslims."

The Saudis, fearing the spread of Iran's Shi'a fundamentalism in the 1980s, began to pour enormous sums into bolstering their Wahhabist tradition. In an ironic twist, they provided the funds for the madrasahs of Pakistan that spawned the Taliban, who later became Osama bin Laden's private army. Every year these religious schools (which number more than 10,000) returned thousands of their graduates not only to Pakistan and Afghanistan but also to the former Soviet states of Central Asia, as well as to Malaysia, Thailand, Indonesia, Sudan, the Philippines, Germany, Italy, the United Kingdom, and the United States. As a result, the number of Wahhabists has been increasing worldwide.

Bin Laden's wealthy and powerful father, who is said to have been fiercely opposed to the presence of Israel in the Middle East, died when Osama was 13.

In 1980 bin Laden received a civil engineering degree from King Abdul-Aziz University in Jeddah, Saudi Arabia. In the early 1980s he joined the Mujahedeen in Afghanistan, but not as a military combatant. Through the Office of Services, which he co-founded (see Chapter 6, "Formula for Terror," for details), Arab recruits were enlisted and transported from 50 countries to fight the Soviets. The Office of Services also set up paramilitary training camps, and bin Laden oversaw the building of roads and hospitals.

The millionaire, who lived as the other Mujahedeen did, spoke softly, and devoted himself completely to restoring the purity of Islam and combating the forces of corruption, soon had a legion of admirers. They couldn't fail to notice that, like the Prophet Muhammad, bin Laden cared nothing for the things of this world and used his wealth for the good of pious Muslims. It was the beginning of his career in terrorism.

In Afghanistan bin Laden formed close relationships with the men who would become leaders of Al Qaeda in 1988 when he formed "the Base." The Soviet withdrawal in 1989 was a heady victory; the Saudis, Egyptians, Algerians, and other Arab Mujahedeen who had fought and defeated the Soviet Union thought they could do anything.

Bin Laden returned to Saudi Arabia and continued to build the Base. The Saudi government cancelled his passport in 1991, and he relocated to Sudan, where he established Al Qaeda training camps and planned terrorist attacks. By 1994 his activities had reached major proportions; the Saudi government revoked his citizenship, and his family disowned him. In Sudan he continued to plan and organize increasingly violent attacks (described in the preceding chapter).

In 1996 Sudan's government, under strong pressure from the United States to expel him, persuaded bin Laden to return to Afghanistan. This, according to a U.S. diplomat, was most unfortunate. "Sending bin Laden back to Afghanistan was like sending Lenin back to Russia," he said. "At least in the Sudan we could monitor some of his activities."

Bin Laden in Afghanistan

In Afghanistan, the newly established government was being besieged by a fundamentalist faction of Pakistani students called the Taliban. Its leader was the one-eyed Mullah Mohammed Omar. Shortly after bin Laden's arrival in Jalalabad with 50 of his family members and hundreds of trained jihad soldiers, he formed a close friendship with Omar and came to share his vision of creating a righteous Islamic system in Afghanistan with students who were steeped in the teachings of the Koran.

The two had much in common. Both were veterans of the war against the Soviets, devout Sunni fundamentalists, and haters of the United States and Israel. Omar, however, was an unlikely leader of a political movement. He was not tall, articulate, and charismatic like bin Laden. He was rather stocky and shy, and he lacked a formal education. Before the war, he had been a peasant preacher in the tiny Afghan village of Singesar.

During the conflict with the Soviets, Omar had distinguished himself as a fearsome fighter, and tales of his exploits circulated among the soldiers. In 1986 he had lost his eye after being hit by shrapnel from a Soviet rocket attack. Omar, according to reports, pulled out a pocketknife and removed the remainder of his eye without uttering a cry or whimper.

Bin Laden provided millions to the ethnic Pashtun Taliban to shore up their efforts to overthrow the ruling minority coalition of Ahmad Shah Massood. Bin Laden also released his own soldiers to the ranks of Omar's troops. This turned the tide of the revolution. By 1998 Omar and his zealots controlled more than 90 percent of the war-ravaged country. In the wake of the victory, Omar married one of bin Laden's daughters and became a member of the bin Laden family.

"Bin Laden controls the Taliban," an FBI official said. "It belongs to his Base, Al Qaeda. That was obvious in 1997 when the Taliban rejected President Clinton's offer to grant the new state international recognition and millions in foreign aid in exchange for the release of bin Laden into U.S. custody. It was an incredible offer. But they turned it down."

While the rebellion in Afghanistan raged, bin Laden continued to orchestrate terrorist attacks throughout the world.

In 1996 there was an attack against the Khobar Towers apartment building that housed U.S. military personnel in Dhahran, Saudi Arabia. The attack resulted in the death of 19 American servicemen. It was executed to impart a univocal message: The United States must withdraw its military bases from the land of the Prophet. In a public statement, bin Laden spoke of the attack as "praiseworthy terrorism," and pledged to conduct similar raids on the U.S. military in Somalia and Yemen.

Many Saudis rejoiced in the actions of Al Qaeda and proclaimed bin Laden a "hero of the people." In private, King Fahd professed his admiration for the terrorist group and, according to one report, even encouraged bin Laden to return to his homeland.

The World Islamic Front

In February 1997 bin Laden announced the creation of a new alliance of terrorist organizations, the World Islamic Front for Jihad Against Jews and Crusaders. The front included such groups as the Egyptian Al-Gama'a al-Islamiyya, the Egyptian Islamic Jihad, and Harakat ul-Ansar.

While the rift between Sunnis and Shi'as continued, bin Laden and Al Qaeda made some headway in forging a union between the traditions in the cause of jihad. In 1998 Al Qaeda members received training from Hizballah, the Iranian-backed Shi'a group in Lebanon, in the art of making car bombs. This was notable because it represented the first attempt by radical factions of both religious parties to work together. In his 1996 "Declaration of War," bin Laden calls upon all Islam—the righteous (Sunni), as well as the unrighteous (Shi'a), to take part in the great struggle against Israel and the United States:

"The ultimate aim of pleasing Allah, raising his word, instituting his religion and obeying and pleasing his messenger (Allah's blessings and salutations on him) is to fight the enemy in every aspect and in a complete manner; if the danger to the religion from not fighting is greater than that of fighting, then it is a duty to fight them even if the intention of some of the fighters is not pure, i.e., fighting for the sake of leadership [personal gain] or if they do not observe some of the rules and commandments of Islam. To repel the greatest of these two dangers on the expense of the lesser one is an Islamic principle which should be observed. It was the tradition of the people of the Sunnah to join and invade—fight—with the righteous and the non-righteous men.

"Allah may support this religion by righteous and on righteous people as told by the Prophet (Allah's blessings and salutations on him). If it is not possible to fight except with the help of non-righteous military personnel and commanders, then there are two possibilities: either fighting will be ignored and the others, who are the great danger to this life and religion, will take control; or to fight with the help of non-righteous rulers and therefore repelling the greatest of these two dangers and implementing most, though not all, of the Islamic laws. The latter option is the right duty to be carried out in these circumstances and in many other similar situations ...."

Osama bin Laden's war was not only with the United States and Israel, but also with many leaders of the Muslim world. In the Al Qaeda manual, several prominent Muslim figures are cursed as infidels and apostates.

Apostates

Al Qaeda targeted Sunni Muslims as the primary enemy of pure Islam for this reason: It is impossible for a Shi'a, who lacks right belief to begin with, to become an apostate. Shi'as must be classified as "nonreligious" and accepted into the fold, along for the sake of the New World Order: the creation of a Muslim utopia. With the Sunni apostates, those of right belief who corrupted Islam, there can be no reconciliation.

In this perspective, the United States could be seen to be, in effect, a secondary target of Al Qaeda's terrorism—the occasion, but not necessarily the cause, of the apostasy of the Sunni leaders.

In several documents, the apostates are identified as follows:

- **Anwar Sadat.** The leading apostate of the twentieth century was the former president of Egypt. His offenses against the faith—in the eyes of Al Qaeda—are egregious and many. He initiated *Infitah* (the "Open Door" policy) that encouraged the financial investments of the United States and other foreign governments in Egyptian business and industry. When faced with pressure from the International Monetary Fund to remove food subsidies for the masses that were sapping Egypt's financial reserves, Sadat abolished the subsidies in 1977 and caused food prices to double and food riots to erupt throughout the country. In 1978 he traveled to Jerusalem to make overtures of peace that resulted in a peace settlement. This made him—in the eyes of the Islamic fundamentalists—a traitor who toadied to Western interests. Egypt, under Sadat's leadership, became the first Arab state to recognize Israel's right to exist. In 1981 Sadat was assassinated at a military parade.

His death elicited little reaction from the Egyptian people, who had poured into the streets to mourn the death of his predecessor, Gamel Abdel Nasser (no hero himself, he had been responsible for their humiliating defeat in the Six Day War with Israel).

- **Hosni Mubarak.** Sadat's successor is high on the Al Qaeda hit list. As soon as he was elected, Mubarak declared his intention of continuing the political policies of Sadat by initiating a reconciliation with the United States and Western leaders and pursuing a path of peace with Israel. This enraged the Egyptian Jihad and other Islamic militant groups, who began to murder foreign tourists. Mubarak responded by taking measures to suppress militant Muslims. To make matters worse in the eyes of Al Qaeda, Mubarak had supported the crushing UN sanctions against Iraq after Iraq took occupation of Kuwait in 1990 and had sent 38,000 Egyptian troops to support the United States and its allies during the Persian Gulf War. In 1997 several members of Al Qaeda launched a failed attempt to assassinate him.

- **Hafez Assad.** He is the exception on the hit list of apostates. An Alawi, and, therefore, a Shi'a, Assad came to power through a coup in 1970 and launched a 30-year reign of terror over the predominantly Sunni population of Syria. While they lived in poverty in a merciless police state, the utterly corrupt and nepotistic Assad and his family plundered the country. In 1982, during a massive Sunni uprising led by Egypt's Muslim Brotherhood, on Assad's order, as many as 30,000 Sunnis were killed by artillery fire in the center of the city of Hama.

- **Ali Abdallah Saleh.** The president of Yemen, he was responsible for rounding up members of Al Qaeda in the wake of the group's attack on the USS *Cole* in Aden

Harbor (which resulted in the deaths of 17 American sailors). Saleh also publicly decried Al Qaeda's kidnapping of 16 European tourists, 4 of whom were killed in a gunfight between the terrorists and Yemeni government troops.

- **Muammar Gaddafi.** At the start of his career as head of the Libyan Arab Republic, Gaddafi was the shining Sunni in the eyes of radical and fundamentalist Muslims. He sought the union of Libya, Egypt, and Syria into a Federation of Arab Republics that would serve to rid the Arab world of Western presence, interests, and influence. He also served as a stalwart supporter of the Palestine Liberation Organization (PLO). His esteem rose even higher when he called for the creation of a Saharan Islamic State and supported anti-government forces in sub-Saharan Africa. By the 1980s Gaddafi became the principal financier of terrorist groups. But he made serious mistakes in the eyes of Al Qaeda. He was scorned for his lack of Islamic credentials and ridiculed for having un-Islamic female guards. He refused to provide open support for Iraq during the Persian Gulf War. He also met with South African president Nelson Mandela and UN Secretary General Kofi Annan to hand over two Libyan terrorists who had been involved in the 1988 explosion of Pan American Flight 103 over Lockerbie, Scotland, which killed 230 passengers.

- **King Fahd Bin Abdul Aziz Al-Saud.** In Al Qaeda's view, the Saudi king is the greatest living apostate. He was influential in establishing OPEC policies that are excessively favorable to the United States, and thereby depleting the natural resources of the land of the Prophet to serve the Kingdom of Satan. When Iraq invaded Kuwait in 1990, King Fahd invited U.S. military forces to the land of Islam's holiest places: Mecca and Medina.

In his 1996 "Declaration of War Against the Americans Occupying the Land of the Two Holy Mosques," bin Laden writes about bringing the young men back to Islam:

> "[The rulers] tried using every means and [kind of] seduction to produce a generation of young men that did not know [anything] except what [the rulers] want, did not say anything except what [the rulers] think about, did not live except according to [the rulers'] way, and did not dress except in [the rulers'] clothes. However, majestic Allah turned their deception back on them, as a large group of these young men who were raised by [the rulers] woke up from their sleep and returned to Allah, regretting and repenting.
>
> "The young men returning to Allah realized that Islam is not just performing rituals but a complete system: religion and government, worship and jihad, ethics and dealing with people, and the Koran and the sword. The bitter situation that the nation has reached is a result of its divergence from Allah's course and his righteous law for all places and time. That bitter situation came about as a result of its children's love for the world, their loathing of death, and their abandonment of jihad."

"In a series of fatwas released from inside Saudi Arabia, prominent Muslim clerics have instructed their followers to wage jihad on Americans in the kingdom and condemned the rulers who give them protection as infidels. The religious edict appears to sanction the overthrow of the house of Al Saud, and makes the royals apostates, subject to the Koranic punishment of death."

—Nicolas Pelham, *Christian Science Monitor,* October 12, 2001

In May 1998 bin Laden announced at a press conference in Afghanistan that the world would witness the results of the new alliance (Al Qaeda) "in a few weeks."

On August 7, 1998, Al Qaeda choreographed simultaneous bombings of U.S. embassies in Nairobi, Kenya, and Dar es-Salaam, Tanzania, killing a total of 301, including 12 American diplomats and government personnel and 38 Foreign Service Nationals. In addition, more than 5,000 were injured.

In retaliation, the United States launched Operation Infinite Reach and bombed the Al-Shifa pharmaceutical plant in Khartoum and a terrorist training camp in Khost, Afghanistan. Officials from the Clinton White House announced that the Al-Shifa facility was not a pharmaceutical plant but a chemical weapons manufacturing complex engaged in the production of the nerve agent VX. A thorough investigation of the site later failed to produce any evidence of chemical weapons production.

In 1999 Al Qaeda attempted to blow up an American ship, the USS *The Sullivans,* as it passed through a harbor in Yemen. The attempt was a fiasco. The ship, loaded with explosives, sank a few feet from the shore. But this setback did not dishearten members of the terrorist group. They had learned from their years of guerilla warfare to turn failure into success.

On October 12, 2000, the same group of Yemeni terrorists who had failed so miserably in their attempt on *The Sullivans* bombed the USS *Cole* in the port of Aden. It was a smashing success; 17 American servicemen were killed.

But the *piece de resistance* of Al Qaeda terrorism was yet to be served to the Great Satan.

On September 11, 2001, Al Qaeda suicide bombers hijacked American Airlines Flight 11 and United Airlines Flight 175 and flew them into the twin towers of the World Trade Center in the financial heart of New York City. The 110-story towers were flattened. It was the worst terrorist attack that had ever taken place on U.S. soil, leaving more than 3,000 people entombed in a massive heap of rubble that became known as Ground Zero.

Shortly afterward, American Airlines Flight 77 careened into the Pentagon, leaving a gaping hole in the nation's hub of military might and killing all 58 passengers aboard the plane and 120 others on the ground.

Within the hour, United Airlines Flight 93 crashed in a field outside Pittsburgh, Pennsylvania, killing everyone on board.

Of the 19 Arabs who perpetrated the attacks, 15 were Saudi Arabian nationals.

It was a nightmare beyond belief.

8

The Reach of Al Qaeda

"In every terrorist act by Al Qaeda since the early 1990s bin Laden has ensured that the actual suicide bombers were 'sleepers,' long-time residents of the countries they attacked, with ordinary jobs, identity papers and a social and family life. Bin Laden has spent a decade building up such networks of individuals, some of whom have never travelled to Afghanistan to meet him."

—Ahmed Rashid, *Daily Telegraph*, September 15, 2001

Mohamed Atta

Mohamed Atta was born in Egypt on September 1, 1968. Fred Williams (not his real name), who met him in Venice, Florida, several weeks before the attack, says that Atta lived in an unassuming apartment in a low-rent district of the city, jogged throughout the neighborhood, and spent time in the local bars. "He seemed like a regular guy," Williams said. "He wore a Nike T-shirt, Tommy Hilfiger jeans, and expensive sunglasses." Williams also recalls that he used expensive cologne, "the kind that sells for $50 a bottle. His English was really good. He hardly had an accent. When I asked him where he was from, he said Hamburg, Germany. I believed him."

Williams says that Atta didn't fit the stereotype of a terrorist. "He didn't wear a turban or anything, and he was clean-shaven. He

(Courtesy FBI)

looked like any other guy. When I first saw him, I thought he might have been Hispanic."

Atta, Williams remembers, spent a great deal of time at the local gym, pumping iron and working out on the exercise machines. "He was a small guy," Williams says, "but he was as strong as an ox. He could bench press 250 pounds, and he couldn't have weighed more than 150. The guy was kind of wiry, like a light-weight boxer."

Mohamed Atta.

(© Getty Images)

Mohamed Atta, informal photo.

But Atta wasn't a boxer, he wasn't a man on the make, and he wasn't from Hamburg, Germany. He was born and raised in Kafr El Sheikh, a small city on the Nile Delta. Mohammed El Amir, Atta's father, is a wealthy lawyer, and his mother is a homemaker who is neither shy and retiring nor dressed in a full burqa. In fact, she doesn't even wear a veil.

The terrorist was born and raised in a spacious house in an upper-class neighborhood. Atta and his sisters attended the best schools in Cairo. One of his sisters became a zoology professor, the other a medical doctor. Atta received a degree in architectural engineering from Cairo University, where he is remembered as a bright and popular student. Quoted in a September 30, 2001, *Time* magazine article, Ahmed Khalifa, Atta's roommate at Cairo University, said, "He was modest in everything. His emotions were steady, and he was not easily influenced or swayed. Mohamed was well-liked because he never bothered anyone." Another classmate quoted in *Time,* an attractive woman named Iman Ismail, said, "He was good to the roots."

In 1992 Atta enrolled at the Technical University of Hamburg, where he hoped to obtain a degree in urban planning. At the university, he befriended fellow student Volker Hauth, and the two traveled and studied together for the next two years. "I knew Mohamed as a guy searching for justice," Hauth told the *Los Angeles Times*. "He felt offended by the direction the world was taking." Another student, who chose to speak anonymously, said, "Mohamed was not an uptight fundamentalist. He liked the girls, but he was very much afraid of getting AIDS or a venereal disease. He loved to go to the spas and to look at the naked women. He wasn't gay or anything."

In 1995 Atta began to work on his thesis, which sought to explore the conflict between Islam and modernity in terms of city planning. To his thesis advisors, Atta expressed dismay over the architecture of Western cities and particularly the rise of skyscrapers in Arab cities.

To research his thesis project, Atta made a trip to Aleppo, Syria, where, according to FBI sources, he came into contact with a prominent Syrian businessman, Mamoun Darkazanli. Darkazanli, it was later learned, had close connections with Osama bin Laden and had power of attorney for a multimillion-dollar bank account in the name of one of the members of the Al Qaeda finance committee.

When Atta returned to Hamburg, almost everything about him had changed. He grew a long, busy beard—the kind favored by fundamentalists—and spent hours poring over the Koran. He grew more reclusive and intense. Chrilla Wendt, who came to know Atta after he returned to the university, said she couldn't remember her classmate ever smiling or making a flippant statement (*Time,* September 30, 2001).

Early in 1999, university officials gave Atta permission to form an Islamic student group. The group came to attract 40 to 50 members who gathered to pray every day. Two of the members of the group were Marwan Al-Shehhi and Ziad Samir Jarrah, who took part in the terrorist attacks of September 11, 2001.

At the end of 1999, several members of the prayer group, including Al-Shehhi and Jarrah, reported to German officials that their passports had been stolen. This was a means of clearing any records of flights to Afghanistan that would have alerted Interpol and the CIA.

On June 2, 2000, Atta arrived at the international airport in Newark, New Jersey, on a plane from Prague with a six-month tourist visa. He and Al-Shehhi began to move ahead with their plan to attack America. They got their pilot's licenses and took Boeing 727 flight simulator training in Florida.

In January 2001, FBI sources assert, Atta flew to the beach resort of Salou in Spain, where he met with Iraqi extremists, military advisors to Saddam Hussein, and the head of the Iraqi intelligence service. Money was transferred by the Iraqi officials to Atta's bank account in Florida. Atta stayed with his Iraqi contacts at the resort for more than a week.

The plans of Atta, Al-Shehhi, and Jarrah, however, now needed approval. For that reason, the same sources say, Atta returned to Spain to meet with Iraqi officials, members of bin Laden's organization, and other terrorist groups. During the 10-day trip, he also made arrangements for another transfer of funds. The year of planning, traveling, and training for the first major assault by terrorists on the United States would cost less than $2,000,000.

Atta returned to southern Florida on a business visa. Four days before he piloted a plane into the World Trade Center, Atta, Al-Shehhi, and another man visited Shuckum's Oyster Bar and Grill in Hollywood, Florida. Contrary to published reports, Atta did not pass the night drinking bottles of beer and shots of whiskey at the bar. Instead, he drank several glasses of cranberry juice and played a pinball machine, Golden Tee '97, for three and a half hours.

The Al Qaeda Fraternity

Intelligence services knew before September 11 that there were many radical Islamic groups in Asia, Africa, and the Far East that had some degree of association with "the Base." Jamal Ahmed al-Fadl told the CIA in 2000 that there were terrorist cells of Al Qaeda and similar Sunni extremist groups in Uzbekistan, Tajikistan, Pakistan, Bangladesh, the Philippines, and Malaysia. There is a cell in Bosnia (that, ironically, came to receive support from the United Nations) and in Chechnya. There is a cell in bin Laden's homeland of Saudi Arabia. There are many African cells, most of whose members are non-Arabs, in Tanzania, Uganda, Kenya, Somalia, Ethiopia, Yemen, Erithea, Egypt, Libya, Algeria, Mauritania, and Sudan.

Al Qaeda cells exist in Germany and (as evidenced by the testimony of Djamel Begal) in England. There is a cell in Montreal, Canada; that became evident by the arrests of Ahmed Ressam and Mokhtar Haouari for plotting to blow up Los Angeles International Airport during the millennium celebrations.

> Ressam told authorities that he planned to plant a suitcase bomb at the airport, but no one else involved in the plot, including Haouari, knew precisely where. The plot was foiled in December 1999 when Ressam was caught trying to enter Washington State from Canada in a car loaded with explosives. During the interrogation, Ressam boasted of the dedication and loyalty of his Al Qaeda associates in Montreal and said that he owed his allegiance not to bin Laden, but to Haydar Abu Doha, a London resident close to bin Laden, who was recently arrested on terrorism conspiracy charges in the United Kingdom.

What was not evident until after September 11, 2001, was the chilling fact that terrorist cells existed in the United States—in Boston, Miami, Chicago, New York, and other cities.

Americans have been involved with Al Qaeda since its inception. Raed Hijazi, an American citizen, is standing trial in Jordan for terrorism. He confessed to planning terrorist attacks and receiving bomb-making training in an Afghan guerilla camp run by bin Laden. One such attack, planned by Hijazi, occurred on Christmas Eve, 1994, when a group of Islamic extremists hijacked an Air France passenger plane with plans to blow it up over Paris. The plane got as far as Marseilles, where it was stormed by Interpol. All but three of the passengers, who were killed, were rescued by the Interpol team.

On September 16, 2001, Secretary of Defense Donald Rumsfeld said that there were Al Qaeda cells active in 60 countries. Since then ...

- German officials have identified five men suspected of assisting Mohamed Atta in Hamburg during his planning of the September 11 attack.
- In Spain, eight men have been linked to the September 11 attack.
- Eleven of the nineteen hijackers are thought to have been in Britain during the nine months prior to the attack.
- The leaders of the hijacking groups spent months in the United States prior to the attack.

When the identities of the hijackers were ascertained, a confusing and unsettling picture of them emerged. They looked like, sounded like, and lived like conventional young men, blending into their surroundings in London, Hamburg, Florida—in any Western country they lived in. How could they be the same men who had slaughtered innocents and were willing—eager—to die in order to kill Americans?

A November 4, 2001, piece in *Time* magazine proposed that Al Qaeda is connected with the extremist Islamic ideology of a group based in Algeria called the Takfiris (*Takfir wal Hijra*), whose members are known to blend into host communities to avoid suspicion. The article quotes a French official as saying that they come across as "regular, fun-loving guys—but they'd slit your throat or bomb your building in a second." Scholars quoted in the piece believe that several high-level Al Qaeda leaders, including Ayman al-Zawahiri, are associated with the Takfiris. In any case, we now know that there are Al Qaeda "sleepers" who hide in plain sight in the United States and in many other countries, waiting to be called to serve Al Qaeda's jihad. Since

September 11, Western governments have made it a top priority to identify these individuals and the cells they are associated with. On December 30, 2001, *The Washington Post* quoted "senior U.S. officials" as stating that "the FBI is conducting more than 150 separate investigations into groups and individuals in the United States with possible ties to Osama bin Laden's Al Qaeda organization."

"German investigators still have more questions than answers about key members of the hijacking team that was based in Hamburg, including presumed leader Mohamed Atta. Counterintelligence officials believe the men went to Hamburg five to eight years ago as faithful but not particularly devout Muslims and were radicalized later. They believe the men must have fallen under the tutelage of a particular imam, but they have not been able to identify such a person. Whoever filled that role presumably played on individual vulnerabilities among the recruits. Atta, for instance, was the son of an overbearing father who thought his only boy wasn't tough enough. The son was deeply uncomfortable with girls, unsure of what he was doing with his life, and suddenly found himself alienated in the beer-swilling student society of Hamburg. At some point he became convinced—or someone convinced him—that he was the personal agent of God Almighty."

—Jeffrey Bartholet, *Newsweek*, October 22, 2001

Muslims in the West, says Olivier Roy (*Charlie Rose*, November 7, 2001), are especially vulnerable to militant Islamic movements. The conflicts within Islam and within Muslim societies can be exaggerated in the minds of Muslims who live as minorities in Western countries. They can feel as if they have no home; Roy thinks that Al Qaeda creates an idealized, imaginary world where their conflicts are resolved.

Estimates vary of the number of men who have graduated from Al Qaeda training camps—from 20,000 to 70,000—and been sent to countries throughout the world to live what appear to be conventional lives while they wait for their orders. Given how much is still unknown about Al Qaeda's complex and highly secret supranational structure, tracking down individuals and cells is likely to be an ongoing process for some time to come.

Al Qaeda's Faithful

Much more is known about the leaders and the leadership structure of Al Qaeda. Through evidence given by Al Qaeda defectors, investigators have identified the individual members of Al Qaeda's ruling body, the Shura Council (discussed in Chapter 1, "Inside Al Qaeda"). In addition, a second tier of individuals has been identified who have taken the oath of allegiance (the bayat) to Osama bin Laden. They remain key figures in the Al Qaeda organization, and those whose photos are included in the following list are on the FBI's list of 22 Most Wanted Terrorists. The following list is contained in *Usama bin Laden's al-Qaida: Profile of a Terrorist Network,* by Yonah Alexander and Michael S. Swetnam (Transnational Publishers, 2001).

- **Ahmed Abdullah.** A terrorist from Yemen who was arrested in Pakistan with two members of Harakat ul-Mujaddem on April 2, 2000.
- **Mustafa Mahmoud Said Ahmed, a.k.a. Shaikh Saiid.** An Egyptian with close ties to Ayman al-Zawahiri ("the Doctor"). He was charged with the bombings of the U.S. Embassy in Tanzania by the Tanzanian Magistrates' Court on September 21, 1999. The Egyptian government has also charged him with terrorist activities, including the kidnapping of tourists. Raised in Zaire, he attended Al Azhar University in Cairo, where he received a degree in agricultural engineering. He worked for the

Kuwaiti Defense Ministry until the Iraqi invasion in 1990. Ahmed returned to Zaire, where he established a training cell for Al Qaeda recruits. In 1994 he relocated to Tanzania, along with Wadih el Hage (who served as one of bin Laden's personal secretaries), and set up a gem business. According to *Time* magazine (November 21, 2001), "Outside bin Laden's inner circle [he is] the most senior figure worrying U.S. investigators …" because he has "the skills and connections to put together funding for another terrorist operation …."

(Courtesy FBI)

Ahmed Mohammed Hamed Ali.

(Courtesy FBI)

Mushin Musa Matwalli Atwah.

■ **Nabil Abu Aukel.** A Palestinian who organized Al Qaeda's first cell in the Palestinian Authority. He underwent advanced training in explosives at bin Laden's Abu Khabab camp in Afghanistan in 1998 and worked closely with Hamas. Aukel was arrested by Israeli authorities in June 2000.

■ **Ahmed Mohammed Hamed Ali.** An Egyptian national, Ali was one of five indicted by a U.S. federal grand jury in December 2000 for the 1998 East African Embassy bombings in Kenya and Tanzania. He reportedly trained the Somali gunmen who killed 18 American servicemen. Ahmed's current whereabouts are unknown.

■ **Mushin Musa Matwalli Atwah.** Atwah, too, was indicted for the 1998 Embassy bombings in both Kenya and Tanzania. He trained Al Qaeda recruits at camps in Sudan, Pakistan, and Afghanistan. He is presently at large.

- **Adel Abdel Bary.** An Egyptian national, Bary ran guest-houses and training camps for Al Qaeda in Afghanistan and Pakistan. He was appointed to head the London cell of the Egyptian Islamic Jihad in 1996 and was a charter member of the group's Advice and Reform Council. Along with Ibrahim Eidarous, he was arrested in London in July 1999 and is currently fighting extradition to the United States, where he faces the death penalty. His fingerprints are on bin Laden's 1998 fatwah, and he has been indicted for both 1998 East African Embassy bombings.

- **Ibrahim Eidarous.** An Egyptian national, Eidarous worked with Bary in the London cell of Al Qaeda. His fingerprints are on letters that claim responsibility for both East African Embassy bombings. Eidarous, who was a member of the Egyptian Islamic Jihad before it merged with Al Qaeda, provided false documentation to several members of the group who traveled throughout Europe, the United States, and the Middle East. As of May 2001, he was in custody in the United Kingdom.

(Courtesy FBI)

Mustafa Mohamed Fadhil.

- **Mustafa Mohamed Fadhil.** Of Kenyan and Egyptian citizenship, Fadhil was indicted for the 1998 bombings of the U.S. embassies in Kenya and Nairobi. He remains at large.

- **Khalid al-Fawwaz.** A key member of the London Al Qaeda cell, al-Fawwaz, a plump, bearded Saudi civil engineer, worked with bin Laden in Afghanistan and traveled with him to Sudan in 1991. He was

dispatched to London to establish a regional office of the Advice and Reformation Committee, which had the job of campaigning for the establishment of Islamic law in Saudi Arabia. Al-Fawwaz, along with his wife, Wejda, both graduates of the King Fahd University in Dharan, were responsible for publicizing the statements of bin Laden and for the procurement of arms and supplies. He were arrested by British authorities in 1998 and awaits extradition to the United States.

(Courtesy FBI)

Ahmed Khalfan Ghailani.

- **Ahmed Khalfan Ghailani.** A Tanzanian national who was indicted for the Embassy bombings. He faces the death penalty if captured.

- **Wadih el Hage.** Born in Lebanon, he attended the University of Southwestern Louisiana, where he received a degree in urban planning. A soft-spoken man with a withered arm, el Hage converted to Islam from Christianity in the 1970s, fought with bin Laden in Afghanistan, and then moved to Tucson, Arizona, where he established a recruiting station for the jihad. When bin Laden moved to Sudan, el Hage picked up stakes to serve as the emir's personal secretary there. Following this stint, el Hage relocated to Nairobi, where he registered with the Kenyan government as a volunteer worker for Africa Help, a humanitarian organization ostensibly based in Hamburg, Germany. He set up several businesses in Kenya as covers for Al Qaeda operations, including Tanzanite King. El Hage also acted as one of bin Laden's scouts for nuclear and chemical weapons. He was arrested by the FBI on September 20, 1998, and remains in custody.

- **Zein-al-Abideen Hussein.** A Palestinian veteran of the Afghan war, Hussein served as coordinator of Al Qaeda's external activities. In this capacity, he was responsible for communications between Al Qaeda headquarters and cells throughout the world. In Peshawar, Pakistan, he screened new recruits for the jihad.

- **Ali Abdelseoud Mohamed.** Even by Al Qaeda's standards, Mohamed's life is extraordinary. While serving as a regular in the Egyptian Army, he wandered into CIA headquarters in Cairo in 1980 and offered his services as a spy. Ali's offer was refused after CIA officials discovered that much of his "inside information" was unreliable. That same year, Mohamed traveled to America under a military exchange program. In 1981 he graduated from the elite Special Forces Officers' School at Fort Bragg, North Carolina, the base for the U.S. Army's Special Operations Command, and was granted the rank of captain in the Egyptian Army. In 1984 he left the Egyptian Army and settled in America on a visa program controlled by the CIA. He enlisted in the U.S. Army in 1986 and received the rank of sergeant and a posting at Fort Bragg. His primary task as a U.S. soldier was to train Muslims to fight the Soviets in Afghanistan. In 1989 he received an honorable discharge from the U.S. Special Forces and traveled to Afghanistan to fight in the jihad. The former American soldier became fast friends with bin Laden. He facilitated bin Laden's relocation from Saudi Arabia to Sudan and later traveled to Canada in order to smuggle terrorists into the United States. He is the only member of Al Qaeda who has pled guilty to the East African Embassy bombings. He is in custody in the United States.

(Courtesy FBI)

Fazul Abdullah Mohammed.

■ **Fazul Abdullah Mohammed.** A dual citizen of the Comoros Islands and Kenya, Mohammed served as a senior aide to Wadih el Hage. The bombs that blew up the U.S. embassies in Kenya and Tanzania were assembled at his residence. He was last seen in the Comoros Islands.

■ **Khalfan Khamis Mohamed.** A Tanzanian national, Mohamed was arrested in Cape Town, South Africa, for his involvement in the East Africa Embassy bombings and was extradited to the United States. In November 2000 Khalfan and Mamdouh Mahmud Salim (a member of Al Qaeda's Shura Council) attempted to escape from the Metropolitan Correctional Center in New York. They stabbed one guard in the eye and another in the stomach before being collared and returned to their cells.

(Courtesy FBI)

Fahid Mohammed Ally Msalam.

■ **Fahid Mohammed Ally Msalam.** A Kenyan national, Msalam is wanted for his involvement in the East Africa Embassy bombings.

■ **Abdallah Nacha.** A Lebanese national, Nacha filmed the U.S. Embassy in Nairobi four days before it was bombed. He was quickly apprehended after the blast. He ran a fish business funded by bin Laden in Nairobi as a front for Al Qaeda activities.

■ **Mohammed Saddiq Odeh.** A Jordanian national, Odeh joined Al Qaeda in 1992. He received training in various camps in Afghanistan. In 1993 he relocated to Somalia to train Islamic troops to oppose U.S. involvement. In 1994 he moved to Mombasa, Kenya, and used Al Qaeda funds to establish a fishing business as a cover. Odeh was arrested in Pakistan the day after the East African Embassy bombings and was extradited to Kenya. He was later turned over to U.S. authorities. He told the FBI that the Kenya bombing was a "blunder," because many Kenyans were killed in the attack.

- **Mohamed Rashed Daoud Al-'Owhali.** An Egyptian national, just before the bomb truck crashed into the U.S. Embassy in Nairobi, he jumped out and threw a stun grenade at security guards. Al-'Owhali was taken into U.S. custody in August 1998 and charged with conspiracy to commit murder, use of a weapon of mass destruction, and 12 counts of murder.

- **Abdurrahman Husain Mohammed Al-Saafani.** Al-Saafani established the first Al Qaeda training cell in Saudi Arabia, where he attempted to smuggle anti-tank missiles into the country and was arrested in 1997. Upon his release, Al-Saafani became involved in the failed attack on the USS *The Sullivans* in January 2000. He remains a prime suspect in the 2000 bombing of the USS *Cole* in Yemen Harbor.

(Courtesy FBI)

- **Sheikh Ahmed Salim Swedan.** A Kenyan national, he was indicted in December 1988 for his involvement in the bombings of the U.S. embassies in Kenya and Tanzania. He remains at large.

Sheikh Ahmed Salim Swedan.

In addition, the following individuals have been identified by the FBI and by Alexander and Swatnam in *Usama bin Laden's al-Qaida* as associates of Al Qaeda:

- **Hamid Aich.** An Algerian, Aich was involved in a plot to smuggle explosives into the United States from Canada.

- **Maulana Masood Azhar.** Released from an Indian prison in 1999, Azhar has led the Jaysh-e-Mohammad, a splinter group of the Harakat ul-Mujahideen.

- **Abdel Salem Boulanouar.** A French Algerian, Boulanouar has ties to Ahmed Ressam, Fateh Kamel, and the Moro Islamic Liberation Front.

- **Bouabide Chamchi.** An Algerian national, Chamchi is a member of the Algerian Armed Islamic Group. He was arrested when he entered the United States with a fake passport in December 1999.

- **Abdelmajid Dahoumane.** An Algerian, Dahoumane is an accomplice of Ahmed Ressam with strong ties to the GIA. He was arrested in Port Angeles, Washington, for his involvement in a plot to blow up Los Angeles International Airport during the celebration of the new millennium.

- **Khalil Sa'id Deek.** A naturalized American of Palestinian descent, Deek was arrested in Jordan for his attempt to bomb the American-owned Radisson Hotel in Amman. Deek detonated the explosives several days after U.S. military commanders left the hotel. The incident resulted in the death of four Australians.

- **Maulana Ghafoor Haideri.** Haideri is the Secretary General of the Jamiat Ulema-e-Islam group with close ties to Al Qaeda. He has bragged that if bin Laden is captured or killed, his group will retaliate against the United States.

- **Mustafa Ahmed Hassan Hamza.** Hamza is a devoted disciple of Ayman al-Zawahiri and traveled with him to Afghanistan to fight in the jihad. For many years he served as the military commander of the Egyptian Islamic Group and participated in the 1981 assassination of Egyptian president Anwar Sadat, the 1995 attempted assassination of President Mubarak, and the attempted assassination of Egyptian Interior Minister Zaki Badr. Hamza was in Khartoum with bin Laden in the early 1990s and later moved to London, a favorite city of the terrorists.

- **Mokhtar Haouari.** An Algerian national and member of the Algerian Armed Islamic Group, Haouari helped establish an Al Qaeda base in Montreal. He has been accused of forging documents to facilitate travel for Al Qaeda members and of planning to bomb Los Angeles International Airport.

- **Raed Mohamed Hassan Hijazi.** Hijazi is an American who was born in California in 1969 and graduated from the California State University in Sacramento. While a college student, he converted to Islam and made several trips to Saudi Arabia and Jordan. From 1997 to 1998 he worked as a taxi driver in Boston, contributing more than $13,000 of his earnings to the Jordanian terrorist group Bayt al-Imam. In 1999 he traveled to Afghanistan, where he received training in explosives and mortars. He was involved in recruiting new members for Al Qaeda in Israel, Turkey, and the United Kingdom, and he purchased large quantities of sulfuric and nitric acid to bomb government buildings in Jordan. He was arrested by Syrian authorities in Damascus and later extradited to Jordan, where he is cooperating with Jordanian officials.

- **Mohamed Ahmed Shawqi el-Islambouli.** This Egyptian national is the brother of Khaled Islambouli, Egyptian president Anwar Sadat's assassin. He is the self-proclaimed protector of Ayman al-Zawahiri and, by all accounts, remains at his side.
- **Eyad Ismail.** A baby-faced Jordanian national, Ismail is a product of higher education in America. He grew up in Dallas, Texas, and later enrolled as a computer student at Kansas University, where he received substantial financial aid. On February 23, 1993, he drove the Ryder truck containing a massive bomb into the World Trade Center in New York, killing six and injuring more than a thousand. On November 13, 1997, he was convicted of terrorism, conspiracy, and murder and sentenced to 240 years in prison.
- **Fateh Kamel.** The former owner of the Aristanat Nord-Sud Craft Store in Montreal, Kamel was arrested in December 1999 for his part in a plot to blow up the subway in Paris. French authorities claim that he is the leader of the Groupe Roubaix, an organization of Islamic bombers and robbers who fund terrorist activities throughout the world.
- **Essam al-Ridi.** A naturalized American born in Egypt, al-Ridi received flight training at schools in Texas and Florida. He served in the war against the Soviets in Afghanistan and became a close friend of bin Laden. During the 1980s he shipped night-vision goggles and rifles to the Mujahedeen. In 1993 he purchased a used jet for bin Laden to transport Stinger antiaircraft missiles from Afghanistan to Khartoum. Al-Ridi also transported hundreds of Afghan veterans to Sudan's Al Qaeda training camps, and he was instrumental in establishing an Al

Qaeda cell in Nairobi. In 1994, after a falling out with bin Laden, he crashed the jet and fled. At the Southern District Court of New York in February 2001, al-Ridi provided information about the inner workings of Al Qaeda and spoke of bin Laden as a "rich man with no military experience trying to be a decision maker."

- **Maulana Fazlur Rehman.** A veteran of the Afghan war, a leader of Harakat ul-Mujahideen, and Secretary-General of the Jamiat Ulema-e-Islam Party in Pakistan, Rehman receives his funding from bin Laden and commands several thousand Afghan warriors. He travels with an entourage of 313 bodyguards who are instructed to kill anyone who might harm him. Rehman was a co-signer of the Al Qaeda fatwa of 1998 and has pledged to attack Americans throughout the Middle East if bin Laden is captured or killed.

- **Ahmed Ressan.** An Algerian and a member of the Armed Islamic Group, Ressan worked with the Groupe Roubaix and Al Qaeda to carry out terrorist activities in and around the town of Roubaix, France. His activities included a shoot-out with an elite French police team in 1996 that left six dead. He is also a prime suspect in the 1996 Port Royal bombing, a subway attack during rush hour that killed 4 and injured 91. The CIA has obtained satellite photographs of Ressam visiting Al Qaeda cells in Afghanistan and Sudan.

- **Hafiz Saeed.** A former professor of Islamic studies in Pakistan, he is the leader of the Lashkar-I-Tayaba, a terrorist group in Kashmir that is funded by bin Laden.

- **Khaled al-Saafani.** Al-Saafani holds both Yemeni and Bosnian passports. He ran a honey business for bin Laden and established an Al Qaeda cell in Kuwait, where he planned to carry out a "big operation." He was collared by the police with a crate of hand grenades and 113 kilos of high explosives.

- **Refai Ahmed Taha.** A leader of the Egyptian Islamic Group, Taha signed the 1998 fatwa and has been sentenced to death in Egypt in the "Returnees from Afghanistan" case. He has been linked to the assassination of Anwar Sadat.

- **Ramzi Ahmed Yousef.** The British-educated Islamic extremist who masterminded the 1993 bombing of the World Trade Center was considered by the FBI for a time to be "the most dangerous man in the world." While on the run from a massive worldwide manhunt, Yousef bombed a Philippines Airlines flight and an Iranian temple. He also made plans to destroy 11 American airplanes over the Pacific, to attack CIA headquarters using a light aircraft armed with chemical weapons, and to assassinate President Bill Clinton, Pope John Paul II, and other world leaders. He was arrested in Pakistan on February 7, 1995, while staying in one of bin Laden's "guest houses" in Peshawar. He was convicted of conspiracy in U.S. federal court on November 12, 1997, and sentenced to life in prison without the possibility of parole.

- **Bakht Zamin.** Head of the al-Badar group in Pakistan, Zamin is a veteran of the Afghan war who has conducted terrorist activities in Kashmir. The group vows to defend bin Laden and Al Qaeda at all costs.

- **Muhammad Rabie al-Zawahiri.** Brother of "the Doctor" and former member of the Egyptian Jihad's Shura Council, he was arrested in the United Arab Emirates in February 2000 and extradited to Egypt, where he was questioned by FBI officials.

As of January 9, 2002, the U.S. State Department's growing list of individuals, groups, and businesses linked to terrorism worldwide numbered 168.

How many individuals throughout the world have "ties" to Al Qaeda? No one knows for sure. The FBI estimate is more than two million of the world's one billion Muslims, but "having ties" could mean as little as having unwittingly contributed to a charitable organization that channeled funds to Al Qaeda. Still, it seems like a preposterously huge number, unless you consider the fact that, in the year 2001, the most popular name for male newborns in the world Muslim community—after Muhammad— was Osama.

9

Jihad

"O prophet Mohammed, urge the believers to fight."
—The Koran (8:65)

"But if the enemy incline towards peace, do thou (also) incline towards peace, and trust in Allah."
—The Koran (8:61)

The term *jihad* means "struggling" or "striving." The struggle referred to in the Koran can mean the internal, personal struggle—to overcome worldly desires or to be a more socially responsible Muslim—or the external struggle—to battle in the cause of Allah or to defend one's land and faith. It is the latter meaning that is more familiar to Westerners, who usually translate *jihad* as "holy war," but most Muslims think of it as striving for a more spiritual and moral way of life. Muslims refer to the internal aspect of jihad as "greater jihad," and to jihad in its militant connotation as "lesser jihad."

In his book *Islam,* Professor Caesar E. Farah makes this distinction: "While the Koran does not make of jihad in the 'holy war' context an article of faith, it is the hadith which renders it into a formula for 'active struggle' that invariably tended toward a militant expression."

"Fighting and warfare might sometimes be necessary, but it was only a minor part of the whole jihad or struggle. A well-known tradition has Muhammad say on returning from a battle 'We return from the little jihad to the great jihad, the more difficult and crucial effort to conquer the forces of evil in oneself and in one's own society in all the details of daily life.'"

—Karen Armstrong, *Muhammad*

Muhammad tolerated the presence of Jewish and Christian enclaves in the Muslim community, granting "the People of the Book (*Ahl al Kitab*)" limited status as members of the community and requiring them to pay a special tax (*jizyah*) applied to *dhimmis* (Ahl al Kitab living under Muslim rule). Pagans, however, the overwhelming majority during Muhammad's time, were dealt with differently; they were required to submit to Islam or suffer the consequences.

Bernard Lewis, in *The Political Language of Islam*, sees the basis of the obligation of jihad as the universality of Muhammad's revelation. Allah's words and messages are for all people, and it is the duty of all those who have submitted to the will of Allah to endeavor (*jihad*) to convert or subjugate all those who have not submitted to the true faith. This obligation is without limit of time and place. It must continue until all of mankind bows toward Mecca for *Salat* (ritual prayer) and cries out in unison: "*Allahu akbar*" (God is greater).

Osama's Jihad

In Al Qaeda's strain of Islam, the world is divided in two: the House of Islam (*Dar al-Islam*), where Muslims rule and the law of the Koran is upheld, and the House of War (*Dar al-Harb*), which comprises the rest of the world. Between these two houses, there can be no peace until Islam triumphs over all unbelief and becomes the universal religion.

It is also proper and necessary, according to Al Qaeda and its network of terrorist organizations, for believers to wage war against apostates—Muslims who have abandoned the faith (discussed in Chapter 7, "Osama bin Laden"). In the eyes of bin Laden, these include the rulers of Saudi Arabia, Egypt, Jordan, Iran, Kuwait, and Libya.

All invocations of jihad must be accompanied by a fatwa or "official" proclamation of all-out war. Because fatwas are based on Islamic law and traditions that *oblige* Muslims to carry them out, throughout Islam's history, they could be issued only by the caliphate (discussed in Chapter 3, "Islam's Sects and Struggles"). Since the caliphate ended with the Ottoman Empire in 1924, fatwas have been considered official only when they are issued by high-level religious authorities or scholars. In recent times, however, their casual employment by terrorist groups has tended to strip the concept of the fatwa of much of its relevance.

Bin Laden's interpretation of jihad is best understood by a reading of the following extended excerpt from his fatwa of February 23, 1996, "Declaration of War Against the Americans Occupying the Land of the Two Holy Mosques":

My Muslim Brothers of the World:

Your brothers in Palestine and in the land of the two Holy Places are calling upon your help and asking you to take part in fighting against the enemy—your enemy and their enemy—the Americans and the Israelis. They are asking you to do whatever you can, with your own means and ability, to expel the enemy, humiliated and defeated, out of the sanctities of Islam ...

O you soldiers of Allah ride and march on! This is the time of hardship, so be tough. And know that your gathering and cooperation in order to liberate the sanctities of Islam is the right step toward unifying the word of the Ummah [Muslim community] under the banner of "No God but Allah."

From our place we raise our palms humbly to Allah asking him to bestow on us His guidance in every aspect of this issue.

Our Lord, we ask you to secure the release of the truthful scholars, Ulama, of Islam and pious youths of the Ummah from their imprisonment, O Allah, strengthen them and help their families.

Our Lord, the people of the cross have come with their horses and occupied the land of the two holy places. And the Zionist Jews are fiddling as they wish with the Al Aqsa Mosque, the route of the ascendance of the messenger of Allah (Allah's blessings and salutations on him). O lord, shatter their gathering, divide them among themselves, shake the earth under their feet and give us control of them. Our Lord, we take refuge in you from their deeds and take you as a shield between them and us.

Our Lord, show us a black day for them!

Our Lord, show us the wonderment of your ability in [defeating] them.

Our Lord, You are the revealer of the Book, director of the clouds. You defeated the Allies (Ahzab); defeat them and make us victorious over them.

Our Lord, you are the one who helps us and you are the one who assists us. With your power, we move, and, by your power, we fight. On you, we rely and you are our cause.

Our Lord, our youth comes together to make your religion victorious and to raise your banner. Our Lord, send them your help and strengthen their hearts.

Our Lord, make the youth of Islam steadfast and descend patience upon them and guide their shots!

Our Lord, unify the Muslims and bestow love among their hearts.

Our Lord, pour down upon us patience, make our steps firm, and assist us against the unbelieving people!

Our Lord, do not lay on us a burden as Thou hast laid on those before us. Our Lord, do not impose upon us that which we have no strength to bear. Thou art our patron, so help us against the unbelieving people.

Our Lord, guide this Ummah, and make the right conditions [by which] the people of your obedience will be in dignity and the people of disobedience in humiliation, and by which the good deeds are enjoined and the bad deeds are forbidden.

Our Lord, bless Muhammad, your slave and messenger, his family and descendants, and companions, and salute him with a [becoming] salutation.

And our last supplication is: All praise is due Allah.

Usamah bin Muhammad bin Laden
Friday, September 4, 1417 A.H.
Hindukush Mountains, Khurasan, Afghanistan

On August 23, 1993, FBI officials interrogated Siddig Ibrahim Siddig Ali, one of the suspects in the World Trade Center bombing and a member of Al Qaeda. During the questioning, Siddig Ali was asked about the significance of the Koran and the teachings of Islam in the attacks. "Of course," he said, "don't forget God said in the Koran, 'in times like this, everything is lawful to the Muslim, [the unbelievers'] money, their women, their honor, everything.' I give you an example: [Egyptian president Hosni] Mubarak, a tyrant. He's killing people, good Muslims. We'll be considered sinners in the eyes of Allah if we don't do something about it. Infidels must be killed! And the Muslim, when he dies, it is the way to heaven. He becomes a martyr. A Muslim will never go to hell by killing an infidel."

According to bin Laden, once the cities of the *harbis* (nonbelievers) have been destroyed, the Muslim terrorists can do what they like with the defeated enemy. Pillage can occur. Rape and murder can ensue. Captives can be cast into prisons or sold as slaves. "Such things will happen in America," Siddig Ali said. "It is the will of Allah."

Laurie Goodstein interviewed several prominent Islamic scholars for a September 30, 2001, piece in *The New York Times* about the role of religion in the September 11 attacks:

"The scholars said that the terrorist acts clearly violated the ethics of battle spelled out by Muhammad. The Koran, which Muslims believe was revealed by God to Muhammad at a time of vicious conflict between Arab tribes in the early seventh century, includes verses that prescribe the rules of war. Like scriptures of every faith, the Koran is open to interpretation and has been twisted to justify the actions of extremists, the scholars said."

In a 1996 interview with the Arabian news agency *Nida'ul Islam,* bin Laden said:

"There were important effects to the explosions on both the internal and external aspects. Most important among these is the awareness of the people [of Saudi Arabia] to the significance of the American occupation of the country of the two sacred mosques, and that the original decrees of the regime are a reflection of the wishes of the American occupiers. So the people became aware that their main problems were caused by the American occupiers and their puppets in the Saudi regime, whether this was from the religious aspect or from other aspects in their everyday lives. The sympathies of the people with the working scholars who had been imprisoned also increased their understanding of their advice and guidance which led the people to support the general rectification movement which is led by the scholars and the callers of Islam. This movement—with the bounty of Allah—is increasing in power and in supporters day after day at the expense of the regime. The sympathy with these missions at the civil and military levels were great, as also the sympathies of the Muslim world with the struggle against the Americans.

"As for the relationship between the regime and the American occupiers, these operations have embarrassed both sides and have led to the exchange of accusations between them. So we have the Americans stating that the causes of the explosions are the bad policies of the regime and the corruption of members of the ruling family, and the regime is accusing the Americans of exceeding their authority by taking advantage of the regime and forcing it to enter into military and civil contracts which are beyond its means, which led to great economic slide which has affected the people. In addition to this is the behavior of the Americans with crudeness and arrogance with the Soviet army and their general behavior with citizens, and with the privileges which the Americans enjoy in distinction from the Saudi forces."

A second reason for the declaration for war, according to bin Laden, was America's barbaric treatment of Muslim people during its war against Saddam Hussein. The bombings of Iraq, bin Laden says, resulted in the killing of thousands of innocent people. In addition, the subsequent blockade resulted in the deaths of "sixty thousand Iraqi children" who were deprived of food and medicine. "You, the USA, together with the Saudi regime," bin Laden argues, "are responsible for the shedding of the blood of these innocent children."

In an interview with John Miller of ABC News in 1998, bin Laden said that the U.S. policy of acts of war against innocent civilians, as evidenced by the bombings of Hiroshima and Nagasaki at the close of World War II, must be met by a similar attack, an attack on U.S. civilians. He told Miller:

> "Each action will solicit a similar reaction. We must use such punishment to keep your evil away from Muslims, Muslim children and women. American history does not distinguish between civilians and military, and not even women and children. They are the ones who used the bombs against Nagasaki. Can these bombs distinguish between infants and military? America does not have a religion that will prevent it from destroying all people."

The third of bin Laden's reasons for the declaration of the jihad is the U.S. support of Israel. In his eyes, Israel represents a renegade state that has robbed Palestinians of their native homeland and subjected them to decades of degradation and persecution. The Jews in Israel also retain control of the third holiest city in Islam—Jerusalem. The Al Aqsa Mosque is in the hands of despised Jews who can only continue their occupation of the Holy Land with the support of the United States. In the interview with Miller, bin Laden said:

"The presence of Americans in the Holy Land supports the Jews and gives them a safe back. The American government, in a time where there are millions of Americans living on the street and below the poverty line, we find the American government turning toward helping Israel in occupying our lands and building settlements in the Holy Land."

A fourth reason for the declaration resides in the U.S. control of Arab oil fields and of the theft of the natural resources of the Muslim people. Bin Laden pointed out that the real reason for the Persian Gulf War was to prevent Saddam Hussein from seizing the rich oil fields of Kuwait. The benefits from the oil fields, bin Laden said in an interview published in *Nida'ul Islam,* flow not to the people of the Middle East, but to the pockets of greedy American capitalists.

In the ABC interview, he told John Miller that to pray is to kill:

"Allah is the one who created us and blessed us with this religion, and orders [us] to carry out the holy struggle— jihad—to raise the word of Allah above all the words of unbelievers. We believe this is a form of worship we must follow despite our financial ability. This is a response to Westerners and secularists in the Arab world who claim the reason for the awakening and the return to Islam is financial difficulties. This is untrue. In fact, the return of the people to Islam is a blessing from Allah and their return is a need for Allah. This is not a strange issue. During the days of jihad, thousands of young men who were well off financially left the Arabian Peninsula and other areas and joined the fighting—hundreds of them were killed in Afghanistan, Bosnia and Chechnya. We pray Allah grants them martyr status."

"[People] ask me about martyrdom. 'Aren't the suicidal hijackers buying a ticket straight to heaven?' Islamic theology, I tell them, is not a business transaction. No one, but no one, knows where they'll end up. Only God knows. Even the Prophet wept with fear that he may not be forgiven. The Islamic doctrine of martyrdom was crystallised in action of Imam Hussain, the grandson of Prophet Muhammad on the battlefield of Kerbala in October 680 A.H. He stood with his 70-odd followers against an army of 4,000 well-equipped soldiers to uphold justice against injustice in the full knowledge that it would cost him his life. His sacrifice was the inevitable consequence of holding firm to what is morally right, not a sought-after, self-chosen, wilful self-sacrifice of one acting beyond any moral or ethical restraint. Suicide hijackers disdain the preciousness of each and everyone of God's creation, themselves and their victims; they cheapen the name of martyr."
—Ziauddin Sardar, *The Observer,* September 16, 2001

In his public statements, bin Laden also has expressed his unshakable conviction, based on these beliefs, that the jihad will result in the utter destruction of the United States.

The superiority of American weaponry and manpower is no match for the rage and faith of the Muslim people. Bin Laden argues that NATO—a "U.S. creation"—has spent more than $4,555 billion for the development of sophisticated weapons to protect Europe and the United States from the Soviet Union, which, by all accounts, was one of the world's two superpowers. NATO, bin Laden says, did not fire a shot to prevent the Soviet takeover of many countries in Eastern Europe. But the Afghan believers in jihad crushed the Soviet Union to such an extent that it remains in ruins. During the ABC interview, bin Laden told Miller:

"The Soviet Union entered in the last week of 1979, in
December, and, with Allah's help, their flag was folded
December 25, a few years later, and thrown in the trash,
and there was nothing left to call Soviet Union .... We
predict a black day for America and the end of the
United States as United States, and will be separate
states. And will retreat from our land and collect the
bodies of its sons back to America."

Al Qaeda is capable of employing a strategy of guerilla warfare
against the United States that will spread terror among U.S. citizens. The weapons of this war will not be directed against armies
and navies but every American man, woman, and child. The
"Declaration of War" says:

"It must be obvious to you that due to the imbalance of
power between our armed forces and the enemy forces, a
suitable means of fighting must be adopted, i.e., using
fast-moving, light forces that work under complete
secrecy—in other words, to initiate a guerilla warfare,
where the sons of the nation and not the military forces
take part in it. And, as you know, it is wise in the present
circumstances, for the armed military forces not to be
engaged in a conventional fighting with the forces of the
Crusader enemy (the exceptions are the bold and the
forceful operations carried out by members of the armed
forces individually, that is, without the movement of the
formal forces in its conventional shape and, hence, the
responses will not be directed, strongly, against the army)
unless a big advantage is likely to be achieved; and great
losses induced on the enemy side (that would shake and
destroy its foundations and infrastructures) that will help
to expel the enemy defeated out of the country ...."

In this war, Al Qaeda will offer no chance for America to come to an agreement with the righteous warriors—no possibility for compromise—no hope for a treaty—no attempt at solution. The war will be waged until the United States remains a memory.

The soldiers and suicide bombers of the jihad are totally committed to their faith and the righteousness of their cause. They know they will be blessed for every American they kill. They love death as Americans love life, because death offers them eternal happiness and the satisfaction of all desire.

The Koran only sanctions martyrdom under very strict conditions such as the struggle against infidels who seize Muslim lands. But it does not condone suicide. Bin Laden, however, maintains that his jihad against the United States is a *defensive* war in which martyrdom is valid, because Americans, by virtue of the presence of U.S. military bases throughout the Middle East, have invaded Muslim lands.

All Islam will be engaged in the jihad. It will attract believers not only from Afghanistan but also Indonesia, Pakistan, India, Bangladesh, Iran, Turkey, Egypt, Nigeria, Morocco, Algeria, China, Sudan, and Iraq. It will be a pan-Islamic phenomenon— a righteous force from many nations and different directions— but all with the same intent.

Because the killing of Americans is a sacred duty, it can be performed by any Muslim at any time in any country in the world.

The World Islamic Front's Jihad

One year after Osama bin Laden's February 1997 announcement of the creation of the World Islamic Front for Jihad Against Jews and Crusaders, the Front issued the following statement, reproduced here in its entirety:

Jihad Against Jews and Crusaders
World Islamic Front Statement
23 February 1998
Shaykh Usamah Bin-Muhammad Bin-Ladin
Ayman al-Zawahiri, amir of the Jihad Group in Egypt
Abu-Yasir Rifa'i Ahmad Taha, Egyptian Islamic Group
Shaykh Mir Hamzah, secretary of the Jamiat-ul-Ulema-e-Pakistan
Fazlul Rahman, amir of the Jihad Movement in Bangladesh

Praise be to God, who revealed the Book, controls the clouds, defeats factionalism, and says in His Book: "But when the forbidden months are past, then fight and slay the pagans wherever ye find them, seize them, beleaguer them, and lie in wait for them in every stratagem (of war)"; and peace be upon our Prophet, Muhammad Bin-'Abdallah, who said: I have been sent with the sword between my hands to ensure that no one but God is worshipped, God who put my livelihood under the shadow of my spear and who inflicts humiliation and scorn on those who disobey my orders.

The Arabian Peninsula has never—since God made it flat, created its desert, and encircled it with seas—been stormed by any forces like the crusader armies spreading in it like locusts, eating its riches and wiping out its plantations. All this is happening at a time in which nations are attacking Muslims like people fighting over a plate of food. In the light of the grave situation and the lack of support, we and you are obliged to discuss current events, and we should all agree on how to settle the matter.

No one argues today about three facts that are known to everyone; we will list them, in order to remind everyone:

First, for over seven years the United States has been occupying the lands of Islam in the holiest of places, the Arabian Peninsula, plundering its riches, dictating to its rulers, humiliating its people, terrorizing its neighbors, and turning its bases in the Peninsula into a spearhead through which to fight the neighboring Muslim peoples.

If some people have in the past argued about the fact of the occupation, all the people of the Peninsula have now acknowledged it. The best proof of this is the Americans' continuing aggression against the Iraqi people using the Peninsula as a staging post, even though all its rulers are against their territories being used to that end, but they are helpless.

Second, despite the great devastation inflicted on the Iraqi people by the crusader-Zionist alliance, and despite the huge number of those killed, which has exceeded one million … Despite all this, the Americans are once again trying to repeat the horrific massacres, as though they are not content with the protracted blockade imposed after the ferocious war or the fragmentation and devastation.

So here they come to annihilate what is left of this people and to humiliate their Muslim neighbors.

Third, if the Americans' aims behind these wars are religious and economic, the aim is also to serve the Jews' petty state and divert attention from its occupation of Jerusalem and murder of Muslims there. The best proof of this is their eagerness to destroy Iraq, the strongest neighboring Arab state, and their endeavor to fragment all the states of the region such as Iraq, Saudi Arabia,

Egypt, and Sudan into paper statelets and through their disunion and weakness to guarantee Israel's survival and the continuation of the brutal crusade occupation of the Peninsula.

All these crimes and sins committed by the Americans are a clear declaration of war on God, his messenger, and Muslims. And ulema [the body of scholars knowledgeable in Islam] have throughout Islamic history unanimously agreed that the jihad is an individual duty if the enemy destroys the Muslim countries. This was revealed by Imam Bin-Qadamah in "Al-Mughni," Imam al-Kisa'i in "Al-Bada'i," al-Qurtubi in his interpretation, and the shaykh of al-Islam in his books, where he said: "As for the fighting to repulse [an enemy], it is aimed at defending sanctity and religion, and it is a duty as agreed [by the ulema]. Nothing is more sacred than belief except repulsing an enemy who is attacking religion and life."

On that basis, and in compliance with God's order, we issue the following fatwa to all Muslims:

The ruling to kill the Americans and their allies and—civilians and military—is an individual duty for every Muslim who can do it in any country in which it is possible to do it, in order to liberate the Al Aqsa Mosque and the holy mosque [Mecca] from their grip, and in order for their armies to move out of all the lands of Islam, defeated and unable to threaten any Muslim. This is in accordance with the words of Almighty God, "and fight the pagans all together as they fight you all together," and "fight them until there is no more tumult or oppression, and there prevail justice and faith in God."

This is in addition to the words of Almighty God: "And why should ye not fight in the cause of God and of those who, being weak, are ill-treated (and oppressed)?—women and children, whose cry is: 'Our Lord, rescue us from this town, whose people are oppressors; and raise for us from thee one who will help!'"

We—with God's help—call on every Muslim who believes in God and wishes to be rewarded to comply with God's order to kill the Americans and plunder their money wherever and whenever they find it. We also call on Muslim ulema, leaders, youths, and soldiers to launch the raid on Satan's U.S. troops and the devil's supporters allying with them, and to displace those who are behind them so that they may learn a lesson.

Almighty God said: "O ye who believe, give your response to God and His Apostle, when He calleth you to that which will give you life. And know that God cometh between a man and his heart, and that it is He to whom ye shall all be gathered."

Almighty God also says: "O ye who believe, what is the matter with you, that when ye are asked to go forth in the cause of God, ye cling so heavily to the earth! Do ye prefer the life of this world to the hereafter? But little is the comfort of this life, as compared with the hereafter. Unless ye go forth, He will punish you with a grievous penalty, and put others in your place; but Him ye would not harm in the least. For God hath power over all things."

Almighty God also says: "So lose no heart, nor fall into despair. For ye must gain mastery if ye are true in faith."

10

The Mind-Set of
a Terrorist

"They [terrorists] are not crazy. Few can be diagnosed
with any disorder found in the American Psychiatric
Association's *Diagnostic and Statistical Manual.* If only
those with some kind of psychopathology could be
terrorists, the problem of terrorism would be trivial."

—Clark McCauley, co-director, Solomon Asch Center
for Study of Ethnopolitical Conflict (interview for a
September 18, 2001, The Why Files)

In the wake of the attack on the World Trade Center in 1993,
months of painstaking investigative work by the FBI established
that it had been carried out by Mohammed Salameh, Mahmoud
Abouhalima, Ahmad Mohammad Ajaj, Eyad Ismail, and Nidal
Ayyad. These Al Qaeda warriors said that they were angered by
the U.S. support of Israel and the corrosive influence of Western
culture on the people of Islam. The men, under the direction of
Ramzi Ahmed Yousef, had constructed a large truck bomb in
New Jersey and transported it to New York. The truck was
parked in a garage under the World Trade Center when the
bomb exploded.

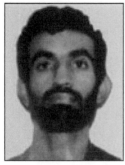

(Courtesy U.S. State Department)

Ramzi Ahmed Yousef.

Shortly after the terrorists were arrested in February 1995, the FBI, with the assistance of Pakistani authorities, were able to collar Yousef in Islamabad, Pakistan, and take custody of him.

Yousef was convicted of the bombing and other crimes in New York Federal Court. He was sentenced to life in prison without parole. The other conspirators received 240-year prison terms.

At his trial, Yousef proclaimed: "Yes, I am a terrorist and proud of it."

Ramzi Ahmed Yousef hails from the Baluchistan province of Pakistan. With the help of bin Laden, Yousef built up a network with direct contact to the Mindanao and Moro Moslem Liberation Armies in the Philippines and with American and European Muslim converts. To secure logistical support for the network, Yousef provided protection along an essential route that drug traffickers and arms dealers used to move their goods out of Afghanistan. The contraband flowed in three directions: north to Chechnya, west to Turkey, and south to the Gulf of Oman. This last route ran along Pakistan's Makran coast and across the Iranian border. Ramzi recruited and trained Sunni militants who infiltrated Shi'a Iran to ensure the flow of drugs and arms to their destinations.

One of Yousef's chief lieutenants was Abdul Hakim Murad, a small, slight man with bushy brown hair who had grown up with him in Pakistan. Murad lived for several years in the United States and attended flight schools in San Antonio, Texas, and Schenectady, New York, before graduating from an academy in North Carolina with a commercial pilot's license.

While Yousef was the subject of an international manhunt, he traveled to Pakistan, where he made plans with Murad to assassinate Prime Minister Benazir Bhutto. The plot backfired, and Yousef and Murad went on to the Philippines, where they made plans to assassinate President Bill Clinton and Pope John Paul II. They were also hatching "the Bojinka Plot," a grandiose scheme to simultaneously destroy 11 American airplanes in flight over the Pacific.

The Bojinka Plot (*bojinka* is Serbo-Croat for "explosion") was to be accomplished with a new type of bomb that was tiny and undetectable. Developed by the ingenious Yousef, the bombs could pass through airport security without raising an eyebrow. The bombs consisted of small amounts of stable liquid nitroglycerine in contact lens cases, and they were designed to be detonated by Casio digital watches that Yousef had rigged as timing devices.

In the Philippines, Yousef and Murad tested the bombs by blowing up a shopping center in Cebu City and the Greenbelt Theater in Manila. A bomb they exploded on a Philippine Airline jet bound for Narita airport in Japan killed one passenger, but the plane landed safely.

While making final preparations for Bojinka, the terrorists met with Terry L. Nichols several times in Cebu City. Nichols, along with Timothy McVeigh, were charged with the bombing of the Alfred P. Murrah Federal Building in Oklahoma City on April 19, 1995, that killed 168 people and wounded another 600. Some FBI officials now believe that Nichols, who has a "mail-order" Filipino wife from Cebu, obtained contact with Yousef through Muslim students at Southwest College in Weatherford, Oklahoma. The officials further believe that Yousef and Murad provided Nichols with training in making and handling bombs. Without such instruction, Nichols and McVeigh would not have been able to assemble a 5,600-pound bomb made of ammonium nitrate and nitromethane. Several informants recently gave testimony that they met Nichols with Yousef in the Philippines and that the American was affectionately known there as "the Farmer."

After the Oklahoma bombing, Murad told prison guards that Yousef's "Liberation Army," a branch of Al Qaeda, was responsible for it. He later made this same claim in writing.

In Manila, several days before D-day for Bojinka, the terrorists spent the night heating and mixing chemicals in a cooking pot. The concoction exploded, and the two men were unable to douse the flames. They fled the scene.

When firefighters and police arrived at the small flat, they discovered containers of sulfuric acid, bomb-making manuals, timing devices, a large photo of the Pope (who was prepared to visit Manila the next day), Bibles, priests' garments, and a map of the route of the Popemobile. Murad was arrested when he returned to retrieve his laptop computer. His desperate act to save the laptop was justified by the fact that it contained all the intricate plans for the bombings of the airliners.

Murad the Casual Killer

Before Murad was extradited for trial in the United States, he was questioned in the Philippines by Manila police officials on January 7, 1995. The terrorist was receptive to questioning because his interrogators were Muslims, and he provided them with some useful information, but that wasn't all: By the time it was over, he had given them a chilling picture of the mind-set of a terrorist.

Interrogator: What will the bomb be made of?

Murad: That will be nitroglycerine.

Interrogator: How will it be made?

Murad: Nitroglycerin. The formula of nitroglycerine would take five of the basic things: 5 milliliters of glycerin, 15 of nitrate, and 22.5 of sulfuric acid, and when we ... when we will mix nitroglycerin, the density of the nitroglycerin is about 1.3, which even you'll put it in the x-ray, you will never, nobody can ...

Interrogator: What will be the container?

Murad: Sorry?

Interrogator: What will be the container?

Murad: What do you mean by container?

Interrogator: Where will you put the nitroglycerin?

Murad: I will take it from here, from the Philippines to Singapore.

Interrogator: Nitroglycerine, it's a liquid?

Murad: A liquid, yeah.

Interrogator: Yeah. So where will you put it? In a bottle?

Murad: You know that contact lenses?

Murad next confided to the interrogators that he intended only to blow up American planes with American tourists, although he and his accomplices were not averse to killing Japanese people because they were not "believers." The interrogators turned the questioning to the business of the terrorists in the Philippines.

Interrogator: What is your plan in the Philippines?

Murad: I'm telling you the truth. I don't have any plans in the Philippines.

Interrogator: How about in the United States?

Murad: I have a lot of plans in the United States. We are planning ... I'm planning to explode this airplane. I have planning of ... I can't breathe! I can't breathe!

Interrogator: What more? What is your plan?

Murad: I have a lot of the United States!

Interrogator: What is your plan in the United States?

Murad: The United States ...

Interrogator: Yes?

Murad: ... killing Americans.

Interrogator: Why? Why?

Murad: That is my ... the best thing. I enjoy it.

Interrogator: What is your plan in America?

Murad: Killing the people there. Teach them ...

Interrogator: How will you kill people?

Murad: I know how ... how to kill people. You can kill them by gas. You can kill them by gun, by knife. You can kill them by explosion. There's many kinds ...

The subject next turned to Murad's ticket for a flight from Manila to Singapore.

Interrogator: What do you do in ... in going to ... Singapore?

Murad: I'll put the bomb in United Air.

Interrogator: United Air?

Murad: Well, I'm planning ... I was planning to go after one week, because there is daily flights from Singapore to Hong Kong and from Hong Kong to Singapore, also daily flights from Los Angeles to Hong Kong ... Singapore.

Interrogator: What do you mean by Liberation Army?

Murad: Liberation Army, as we shall liberate all the Muslims from the United States, from Israel.

Interrogator: Why?

Murad: Because the United States is the first country in this world making trouble for Muslims and for our people.

Interrogator: Making trouble with your country?

Murad: Yes.

Interrogator: What trouble?

Murad: I'm not ... I'm not looking for a country. I don't care about country. We are Muslims. The United States is making trouble for Muslims.

The interrogators proceeded to ask Murad about his passport and his recent trips from the United Arab Emirates to London; from London to Saudi Arabia; from Saudi Arabia to London; from London to San Antonio, Texas; and from Texas to Manila. Finding his answers elusive, they asked him about the Bibles, clerical vestments, and other Christian articles in his possession.

Interrogator: The crucifix.

Murad: What do you mean "crucifix"?

Interrogator: I mean, did you buy it? Did they sell the crucifix? The cross, cross ...

Murad: Cross? Ah, that's a good question. When they open that ... the bags ... we'll put the Bibles and the cross.

Interrogator: Inside the bags?

Murad: Inside the bags. They will think that we are Christians.

Interrogator: What's the purpose of the pictures of the Pope?

Murad: Also to put it in bags and briefcase.

Interrogator: You rented a gown, a vestment, a priest's vestment?

Murad: The dress of a priest.

Interrogator: Yes, with a white collar?

Murad: No, no. I don't know about that. We don't have anything with the Pope. Our enemy is the United States and Israel.

Interrogator: So what organization do you belong to?

Murad: We are from Liberation Army.

Interrogator: What kind? Liberation Army of what?

Murad: Liberation Army. This is the name of our organization.

Interrogator: What?

Murad: Islamic Liberation Army.

The interrogators went on to ask Murad about the "heater" (a semi-automatic weapon) in his possession.

Murad: I don't have anything to do in the Philippines.

Interrogator: You have everything to do with this country. You are here.

Murad: I'm just taking the explosion to Singapore. I don't have anything here.

Interrogator: What's the heater for?

Murad: I was to take it to ...

Interrogator: What?

Murad: I was planning also to go to Paris.

Interrogator: Paris?

Murad: Yes.

Interrogator: Now we are going to Paris? What for?

Murad: What for? To kill people there also.

The interrogators were astonished at the matter-of-fact manner in which Murad made this admission. One of them commented that he said this as casually as if he were going "to collect tickets at a sporting event."

What was Murad thinking when he embarked on his global bombing spree? It was not on the FBI's agenda to try to answer that question.

What thoughts run through the head of a suicide bomber before he engages on a mission to hijack airplanes and kill thousands of civilians? Is he programmed to act like Laurence Harvey in *The Manchurian Candidate*, a brainwashed automaton at the command of Osama bin Laden? Or is he acting out of some inner rage or a deep-seated political conviction? What, for him, is the purpose of his action? Is his act of mass destruction just a random act of nihilism? Or is the act aimed at a higher goal, even a greater good? A partial answer to such questions can be found in a letter uncovered by FBI agents in the luggage of Mohamed Atta, who flew the first plane into the World Trade Center on September 11, 2001.

The Farewell Letter

After Mohamed Atta perished in flames, the FBI found letters in the luggage of the terrorists who had piloted three of the four doomed flights. Some agents believe that one of them was written by Mohamed Atta and distributed to his compatriots during his last meeting with them in Las Vegas. Whatever personal or psychological motivation may have formed the basis for Atta's act of terror, in the letter he left behind, he speaks as a man who was elated at the prospect of serving the will of Allah by destroying the World Trade Center.

"The Prophet said 'He who commits suicide by throttling shall keep on throttling himself in the Hell Fire
(forever) and he who commits suicide by stabbing
himself shall keep on stabbing himself in the Hell
Fire.'"
—Sahih Bukhari, Hadith 2.445, 2.446
"Let those who fight in the cause of Allah sell the life
of this world for The Hereafter. To him who fights
in the cause of Allah—whether he is Slain or gets
victory—soon shall we give him a reward of great
value."
—The Koran (4:74)
The Koran reserves the most extreme punishment in hell
for Muslims who take their own lives. Those who give
their lives in battle while defending Islam, however, are
martyrs and will have a special place in paradise.

Atta's letter begins by offering the following first phase of instructions:

1. Renew your covenant with God.

2. Know all aspects of the plan very well and expect the
   reaction and resistance from your enemy.

3. Read the chapter of the "Tobah" from the Koran.

4. Think about what God has promised the good believers
   and martyrs. Remind yourself to listen and obey that
   night because you will be exposed to crucial situations
   (100 percent). Train and convince yourself to do that.
   God narrated: "Obey God and his messenger and fall
   into no disputes lest you lose heart and your power
   depart and be patient and preserving for God is with
   those who are patient." (The Koran, 8:46)

5. Increase your supplications to God with regard to aid and stability and victory in order to facilitate your matters and shield you from harm.

6. Increase your supplications to God and know that the best way to do so is by reciting the Koran. This is the consensus of all Islamic scholars and it's sufficient that this is the word of God, the Creator of the earth and the Heavens.

7. Cleanse your heart and purify it and forget everything involving this secular life, for the time of playing is gone and it is now truth for truth. How much of our lives have we lost? Should not we use these hours that we have to perform acts of nearness and obedience to God?

8. Let your chest be open because it's only moments before you begin a happy life and eternal bliss with the Prophet and the veracious and martyrs and the righteous and these are the best of companions. We ask God of His bounties and be optimistic because the Prophet was optimistic in all his matters.

9. Establish your goal as one to become patient and to know how to behave and be steadfast and not to know that what's going to hit you would not have missed you and what has missed you would not have hit you. This is a test from God the Almighty to raise you up high and to forgive your sins. You must acknowledge that these are only moments in which you will be raised with gratitude from God, the Almighty, with rewards. "Did you think that you would enter paradise without God testing those of you who struggled in his cause and remained steadfast?" (3:160)

10. Also remember the sayings of God in which he stated: "You did indeed wish for death before you met it. Now

you have seen it with your own eyes and you flinch."
(3:143) "How often, by God's will has a small force vanquished a large one?" (2:249) "If God helps you, none
can overcome you and if He forsakes you, who is there
after that that can help you? In God, then, let the believers place their trust." (3:160)

11. Remind yourself of the supplications and ponder their
    implications during the morning and the evening, etc.

12. Say your supplications and blow your breath on yourself
    and on your belongings (luggage, clothes, knife, ID,
    passport, and all your documents).

13. Inspect your arm ... prior to your departure, "Let one of
    you sharpen your blade and let him ease his sacrifice."

14. Tie your clothes around you in the same way our good
    forefathers had done before you. Wear tight socks that
    would hold on your shoes and won't allow your shoes to
    slip off. These precautions we are expected to follow.
    God is our sufficiency, how excellent a trustee!

15. Pray your morning prayers with a group and think of the
    reward while reciting your supplications and never leave
    your apartment without ablution. "Did you then think
    that we had created you in jest and that you would not
    be brought back to us for account." (23:115)

16. Shave and wash yourself.

The document does not read like a political manifesto or an
expression of rage, but rather like a religious tract that is meant,
not to further a cause, but to fortify faith.

Atta goes on to offer the second phase of preparations for
the attack on America.

After this, the second stage begins:

"If the taxi takes you to the airport, repeat the supplication one should recite upon riding a vehicle and upon entering a city or any other place you enter. Smile and be at peace with yourself because God is with the believers and because the angels guard you even though you may not be aware. God is mightier than all his creations.

"'Oh God, suffice them with whatever you wish.' And say, 'Oh God, put a barrier in front of them and a barrier behind them and further cover them up so that they cannot see.' (35:9) And say, 'God is our sufficiency, how excellent a trustee,' remembering his word most high.

"'Men say to them: "A great army is gathering against you so fear them," but it only increased their faith, they said: "God is our sufficiency, how excellent a trustee."' (3:173)

"After you say these verses, you will notice that things will go smooth as God has promised his servants of his bounties that they will never be harmed as long as they follow the instructions of God.

"'And they returned with grace and bounty from God: No harm ever touched them; for they followed the good pleasure of God and God is the lord of bounties unbounded. It is only the evil one that suggests to you, the fear of his friends. Be you not afraid of them, but fear me if you have faith.' (3:175)

"The real fear is the fear of God because none knows it except the believers. It is he, the one and only, who has everything in his hand. It is the believers who are most certain that God will nullify the plots of the unbelievers. 'That is because God is he who makes feeble the plans and strategies of the unbelievers.' (8:18)

"You have to know that the best invocation is to not let others notice that you are invoking, because if you say it for 1,000 times no one will be aware whether you are only silent or invoking. Even when you say, 'No God but Allah' while you are smiling and reflecting upon it, then it becomes the greatest word. And it suffices that it is the statement of unity, which you have accepted as the Prophet Muhammad (peace and blessings be upon him) and the companions from their time until the day of judgment.

"Don't manifest any hesitation and control yourself and be joyful with ease, because you are embarking upon a mission that God is pleased with. And you will be rewarded by living with the inhabitants of heaven. 'Smile to hardship, O youth, because you are on you way to paradise!' In other words, any action you perform, and any invocation you repeat, God will be with you and the believers to protect them and grant them success and enable them to achieve victory."

The third and final phase of instructions provided guidelines for the terrorists when they boarded the planes:

"When you board the plane, remember that this is a battle in the sake of God, which is worth the whole world and all that is in it, as the Messenger (peace and blessings be unto him) has said.

"And when you sit in your seat, invoke the known supplications, and then be confidant with the remembrance of God. 'O you who believe, if you meet an army, then be confident with the remembrance of God: O you, who believe, if you meet an army, then stand firm and invoke God much so that you may prosper.' (8:45)

"And when the plane takes off, remember the supplications of travels, for you are traveling to God, and what a beautiful travel!

"This will be the hour. Then ask God Most High as he said in his book: 'Our Lord, pour constantly on us and make our steps firm, help us against those who reject faith.' (2:250) And his saying: 'O Lord, forgive us our sins, and anything we may have done that transgressed our duty. Establish our feet firmly, and help us against those that resist faith.' (3:47)

"And remember the saying of our Prophet (peace and blessings be unto him): 'O God, revealer of the Book and mover of the clouds and defeater of the party, defeat them and make us victorious over them.' Supplicate for you and your brothers, all of them, to be victorious, and do not be afraid. Ask God to grant you martyrdom, marching ahead, and not turning back, and be steadfast.

"Let everyone be prepared to undertake his task in a way pleasing to God, and be courageous, as our forefathers did when they came to battle. And, in the engagement, strike the strike of the heroes, as those who don't want to go back to this life, and say: 'God is greatest,' because it plants fear in the hearts of the unbelievers. God said: 'Smite above their necks and smite off their fingertips.' (8:12)

"And know that the Gardens of Paradise are beautified with its best ornaments, and its inhabitants are calling you. Do not let differences come between you. Listen and obey. And if you kill, then kill completely, because this is the way of the Chosen One.

"On no condition [believe] there is something greater
than paying attention to the enemy or attacking him,
because the harm in this is much greater. For the priority
of the group is much more important, since this is the
duty of your mission. Don't take revenge for yourself
only, but make your strike and everything on the basis of
doing it for the sake of God. As an example, Ali ibn abi
Talib (may God be pleased with him) fought with an
enemy among the infidels who spat on him, and Ali
took his sword and did not strike him. When the war
ended, the companions asked him why he did not strike
that person, so he said: 'When he spat on me, I was
afraid to strike him out of egoistic revenge for myself, so
I pulled my sword out. I wanted this to be for the sake
of God.' Then apply the way of taking captives, and do
what God said in his book: 'It is not fitting for a Prophet
that he should have prisoners of war until he has thor-
oughly subdued the land. You look for the temporal
goods of this world, but God looks to the Hereafter, and
God is mighty and wise.' (8:67)

"Let each of you then tap on the shoulder of his
brother … and remind each other that this work is
for the sake of God and do not be afraid. And give him
glad tidings, encourage each other [scratched-out word].
And how beautiful it would be if one read some verses of
the Koran, such as, 'Let those fight in the cause of God
who sell the life of this world for the Hereafter.' (3:74)
And: 'Say not of those who are slain in the way of God,
"They are dead," no, they are living.' (2:164) And other
similar verses that our forefathers used to mention in the
battlefield, so that they bring peace to their brothers, and
make tranquility and happiness enter their hearts.

"Do not forget to take some booty, even if it be a cup
of water with which you drink and offer your brothers
to drink, if possible. And then when the zero-hour
comes, open your chest and welcome death in the cause
of God, always remembering your prayers to ease your
mission before the goal in seconds. And let your last
words be, 'There is no God but Allah, and Muhammad
is his Prophet.' And then comes the meeting in the
Highest Paradise with the mercy of God. When you see
the masses of the infidels, remember those parties that
numbered about 10,000 and how God granted victory
to the believers. God said: 'When the believers saw the
confederate forces, they said, "This is what God and his
Messenger promised, and God and his Messenger told us
what was true."'"

Mohamed Atta came from a privileged Cairo family, and when
he was 24, went to Hamburg to study urban planning. Friends
who knew him in Cairo and during his first few years at
Hamburg's Technical University thought of him as a good guy
and basically unremarkable. At what point was Atta set on a
course that ended in his death as a suicide pilot? What was he
thinking when he piloted American Airlines Flight 11 into the
north tower of the World Trade Center?

What could account for Murad's lack of focus and his icy
distance from the consequences of his acts? Was the interlude
Yousef and Murad shared just a twist on spree killing?

There are many psychologists and terrorism experts whose
stock in trade it is to explore the mind-set of the terrorist who
takes innocent lives, and often his or her own, in the name of a
cause. Leaving aside the question of what goes on in the mind of
bin Laden or al-Zawahiri or the other Al Qaeda leaders, which

for specialists in terrorist psychology is another subject, some of the field's most authoritative voices offer the following speculations about the mind-set of the men who execute Al Qaeda's attacks:

- Dr. Colin A. Ross thinks that a form of mind control, in which religious fanaticism is the primary instrument of control, could have been used on the September 11 hijackers. (Ross Institute, "Thoughts on Terrorism," September 13, 2001)

- Rona Fields, a psychologist who has been psychologically testing terrorists and paramilitaries for 30 years, thinks that "Their definition of right and wrong is very black and white, and is directed by an authoritative director. There's a total limitation of the capacity to think for themselves." She adds that "They believe there's a difference between right and wrong, but when they do something in the name of the cause, it's justified." (The Why Files, September 20, 2001)

- David Long, former assistant director of the State Department's Office of Counter Terrorism, wrote in *The Anatomy of Terrorism,* "No comparative work on terrorist psychology has ever succeeded in revealing a particular psychological type or uniform terrorist mind-set."

- Dr. Aaron T. Beck, author of *Prisoners of Hate,* wrote that "… terrorists who execute well-planned acts of destruction are not deranged … disciplined terrorists such as those who assaulted the structures in New York and Washington are not necessarily filled with rage. They are cold and calculating in carrying out their grand design and are relatively indifferent to their victims. For them, the end justifies the means."

- In *Newsweek* (October 22, 2001), Jeffery Bartholet wrote "Bin Laden is handsome in his way, and he knows which chords to strike. He appeals to a pervasive sense of humiliation and powerlessness in Islamic countries .... Like any fanatic, he makes the world simple for people who are otherwise confused, and gives them a sense of mission."

- In response to the question "How can normal people hurt and kill innocent others?" Clark McCauley, co-director of the Solomon Asch Center, said (September 18, 2001) "The same way that men have been doing these things forever: For cause and comrades, that is, with a combination of ideology and intense small-group dynamics ...."

There may be no simple answer to the question of why so many young men have been eager for the opportunity to carry out Al Qaeda's barbaric attacks, but there is little doubt that bin Laden's incessant invocation of the more militant words of the Prophet Muhammad engaged many in Al Qaeda's cause.

11

Heroin, Cash, and Weapons

"*The Financial Times* notes that '147 Islamist organizations, many of them linked to bin Laden, can draw on funds estimated at between $5 billion and $16 billion.' Bin Laden's take from one source alone—the Afghan drug trade—was $1 billion a year. These facts, coupled with increasing evidence of technical notes, plans and documents obtained from 'safe houses' in Kabul, suggest that Al Qaeda has the interest and the capability to acquire or build weapons of mass destruction."
—Fareed Zakaria, *Newsweek*, December 6, 2001

The speaker is Ali Abul Nazzar. He is 35 years old and deeply tanned. He wears a white Islamic skull cap called a *taqiyyah* and a hooded black cloak called a burnoose, or *selham*. It is early in 2001. In an FBI interview, he is speaking about Osama bin Laden and his association with Al Qaeda.

"The money comes from heroin—not from Emir bin Laden's personal holdings. The United States can freeze all of his assets in every bank and brokerage house and the money will continue to flow into his organization." Nazzar knows the locations of all of the emir's accounts in Malaysia, Hong Kong, Dubai, and Barclays Bank in London.

Nazzar lights a cigarette and inhales deeply. Smoking is forbidden for members of Al Qaeda except when they are serving as "submarines" in enemy territory. "The media keep writing about the emir's construction companies, his currency trading firms, and the Themar al-Mirbaraka Company that grows sesame and white corn. They want people to believe that Al Qaeda is dependent on sesame seeds and personal savings. Of course, this is ridiculous."

Heroin and the Taliban

There seems to be contempt in Nazzar's smile. "The emir [bin Laden] controls it. He is the world's largest supplier. Everyone knows this. His laboratories in Afghanistan produce between 4,000 and 5,000 metric tons of heroin a year. How are you going to touch him? He gets richer with every drug deal made on every street corner. And heroin, as we all know, is the United States drug of choice. It's ironic, isn't it? The emir is fueled by Western decadence."

According to an October 12, 2001, UN report, the Taliban announced that its ban on poppy cultivation had reduced the poppy harvest from 3,276 tons of raw opium in 2000 to 185 tons in 2001. But the flow of opium to international drug markets was unabated, and the price of heroin remained stabilized in Europe and the United States. Some UN officials attributed the continuation of the heroin flow to the emptying of stockpiles onto the market. But other officials claim that the Taliban ban was simply "window-dressing," and poppy cultivation had never ceased. This claim is supported by the fact that the bombing of opium fields in Afghanistan by the United States–led coalition had an immediate impact on the heroin market. In the Green Market of Dushanbe, Turkey, one of the most notorious bazaars in the world, opium was in short supply by the end of October 2001 and the price of heroin had skyrocketed by 50 to 100 percent.

The laboratories, Nazzar says, are necessary. Before they were established, the Golden Crescent of Iran, Pakistan, and Afghanistan could produce only low-grade Number Three heroin, which was only good for smoking. The market called for Number Four, which could be injected, but it could only be produced by consummately skilled chemists working in sophisticated laboratories. Bin Laden knew that Number Four heroin was worth a hundred times the amount of Number Three. For that reason, he created the necessary facilities and recruited chemists from the former Soviet Union.

Nazzar knew the locations of many of the laboratories and had charted the flow of narcotics from Afghanistan to the seaport city of Sofia in Turkey, where it was sold by the *babas* (Turkish drug dealers) to agents of the Sicilian Mafia for distribution throughout the world. Everything came together at Sofia, where the wheelers and dealers of the drug trade resided in comfortable villas or government guesthouses.

"The drug dealers reside openly in Sofia, maintaining flamboyant and free-spending lifestyles," John Lawn, the former director of the DEA (Drug Enforcement Administration), told a Congressional committee in 1998. "Their presence is so obvious and their deals so flagrant that it is impossible not to conclude that they are enjoying official protection."

Producing and refining has been the task of the Afghans, according to FBI sources, and selling and distributing has been the task of the Mafia. While the heroin market is thriving in the United States and Canada, it is booming beyond belief in Europe. The Europeans consume more than 15 tons of heroin a year—twice the amount that is sold in the United States.

"'Terrorism, organized crime and the illegal drug trade are one interrelated problem,' Abdurahim Kakharov, a deputy interior minister of Tajikistan, said at the drug meeting last year. 'The terrorist groups and drugs were exported from the same source'—Afghanistan."

—*The Washington Post*, September 7, 2001

In his interview, Nazzar says that the primary source of the drugs is the Taliban and points out that it is controlled by the emir—Osama bin Laden—and Al Qaeda. He adds that members of Al Qaeda and other "jihad organizations" never indulge in smoking or shooting up heroin. It's for decadent Westerners, to dull their senses before the terrorist attacks and the fall of the Great Satan (the United States). He says that members of the group are not, however, averse to smoking hashish, even opium-treated hashish. It serves to increase their sense of peace before a suicide mission.

The babas and the Mafiosi met in the Hotel Vitosha, a swanky establishment in a Turkish seaport where the dons connected with the babas. Business was conducted in style by men with $200 haircuts, specially designed and tailored Oleg Cassini suits, Valentino ties, Saks Fifth Avenue socks, and Gucci shoes. The fingernails of the Mafiosi and the babas were perfectly manicured, and they wore $30,000 Piaget watches.

Nazzar knew this because he had made many visits to the Hotel Vitosha as a member of the Shura Council (the leadership) of Al Qaeda and the paymaster of the organization. He spoke of a Mafioso named Vinnie Napoli, who represented Lucian Liggio, Salvatore Riina, and Bernardo Provenzano of Corleone; Nitto Santapaolo and the Ferrara brothers from Catania; and other Sicilian crime clans. Napoli, on behalf of the Sicilian crime family, was instrumental in making a connection with the Gambino crime family in New York to import 20 kilos of heroin a month from Afghanistan. This amounted to a quarter of a ton a year, or 5 million fixes at $300 to $500 a fix for prime Number Four.

Funding Al Qaeda

The primary sources of Al Qaeda's funding have been ...

■ The sale of drugs, primarily opiates, through organized crime connections.

■ Contributions from Saudi Arabia. According to a July 7, 1999, article in the *Boston Globe,* in 1999 the Saudi government uncovered $50 million in donations to Al Qaeda from a group of Islamic men of religion.

The terrorist organization also received sizeable funds from the Dubai Islamic Bank, which is controlled by the United Arab Emirates. The Saudi government has detained Khalid bin Mahfouz, a wealthy Saudi banker, for laundering more than $40 million from leading Saudi businessmen through his bank.

The United States has identified a growing number of charitable (that is, tax-exempt) organizations, such as the Mercy International Relief Agency, that raise millions for Al Qaeda.

■ Tribute money paid by Middle Eastern countries to keep Al Qaeda from establishing cells within their borders.

■ Assets from bin Laden's personal fortune, estimated at at least $25 million. The terrorist leader received a sizeable fortune from his father's estate and also made several very shrewd investments. In the Sudan, he established Al Hijra Construction, a firm that received several high-profile contracts from the Sudanese government. He also amassed millions from two investment companies, Taba Investments and Ladin International; al Themar al Mubaraska, an agricultural company that grew to corner the export market on honey, sesame, and corn products; Khartoum Tannery, a leather company; and Qudarat Transport Company.

The United States and other countries have taken steps to track down and freeze funds in bank accounts connected with Al Qaeda, and new legislation has been passed to regulate money-laundering through conventional accounts and *hawalas*, traditional Middle Eastern systems of transferring funds internationally without documentation. The agencies involved are quick to admit, however, that their power to weaken Al Qaeda financially is limited because the group uses other nontraditional ways to move funds, for example, using couriers to move cash or diamonds. Still, the forensic accounting effort is very useful in providing law enforcement with leads to people who have been connected with or have financially aided Al Qaeda.

Conventional Weapons

As the cash flowed in from Muslim supporters and the sale of drugs, the commanders of Al Qaeda began to spend millions on arms to complement the stockpiles of weapons the Russians had abandoned or lost during their 10 years of warfare in Afghanistan, and the weapons that had been provided to the Mujahedeen by the CIA.

Most of Al Qaeda's arms were purchased at the Smuggler's Bazaar in Darra, 20 miles east of Peshawar, Pakistan. Although Darra officially remains closed to tourists, it was, until the recent war on terrorism, a haven for arms dealers. Here you could buy an AK-47 for $200. Bin Laden and his boys preferred the Chinese-made assault versions, because their barrels don't heat up as much and they can be concealed under a *shwaler qamiz* (long white robe). The Chinese assault weapons sold at anywhere from $375 to $1,000.

There were other bargains at the bazaar. Chinese and Russian rocket launchers sold for under $1,000, and rockets by the case went for 400 rupees ($125) each. Here grenades were cheaper than pineapples in American supermarkets. Other bargain items included land mines, antiaircraft guns, bazookas, organ-style self-propelled rocket launchers, and Russian T-55 tanks.

When it comes to arms, Afghanistan may have more guns per capita than anyplace else on Earth.

Along with the weapons came various technological trinkets. In 1992 bin Laden acquired an $80,000 satellite phone from Germany but later ditched it when he discovered that all calls from the phone were monitored by U.S. agents. Bin Laden also purchased a small corporate jet for $210,000 from Essam al-Ridi, a naturalized American from Egypt, who had been trained at a Texas flight school.

Nuclear Weapons

President Bush announced on December 20, 2001, that he had moved to freeze the finances of Umma Tameer-e-Nau, a group established by a former Pakistani atomic energy commission official, for giving nuclear weapons information to Al Qaeda.

According to Arab and Israeli sources, bin Laden's search for nuclear weapons began in 1988 when he employed a team of five nuclear scientists from Turkmenistan, who "used to work on the atomic reactor of Iraq before it was destroyed by Israel in the 1980s." The same sources say that this team of scientists was working to develop a nuclear reactor that could be used "to transform a very small amount of material that could be placed in a package smaller than a backpack."

By 1990 bin Laden had hired hundreds of atomic scientists from the former Soviet Union for $2,000 a month—an amount far greater than their wages in the former Soviet republics. They worked in a highly sophisticated and well-fortified laboratory in Kandahar, Afghanistan.

Bin Laden's search for nuclear weapons continued throughout the 1990s.

Jamal Ahmed al-Fadl, later a CIA source, said that in 1993 he purchased for bin Laden a cylinder of weapons-grade uranium from a former Sudanese government minister who represented "businessmen" from South Africa. Mogadem Salah Abd Al-Mobruk, a lieutenant colonel in the Sudanese Army, had served as Sudan's minister of justice during the Numeiri presidency (1969–1983). The sale, al-Fadl said, was made in the office of the Ikhlak Company in the Barake Building in Khartoum. The purchase price was $1.5 million, and the uranium was tested at a facility in Hilat Koko in Cyprus and later transported to Afghanistan.

Al-Fadl received $10,000 in cash for brokering the deal, but thinking that he'd been underpaid, he stole funds from the emir's bank accounts and made his getaway. He said that at the time, the commanders of Al Qaeda were in the process of purchasing "nuclear suitcases" developed for the KGB, from the Russian Mafia in Chechnya.

Boris and Alexy are affiliated with the Russian Mafia. They work for a former KGB agent named David (these are not their real names) who, after the break-up of the Soviet Union, sold weapons from the Russian arsenal in Chechnya. A sale David made in 1996 made him a wealthy man—so wealthy that he moved his entire operation to New York—so wealthy that he obtained green cards for his associates by arranging marriages for them to women who had obtained American citizenship.

Alexy and Boris say that the deal that made the former KGB agent rich was with "Afghani Arabs" in search of nuclear weapons.

Having secured one source of uranium, bin Laden sought another. On September 25, 1998, Mamdouh Mahmud Salim was arrested in Munich and charged with acting as an Al Qaeda agent to purchase highly enriched uranium from a German laboratory.

In August 1998 bin Laden paid £2 million to a middle man in Kazakhstan to make a deal to buy "nuclear suitcases" from former KGB agents. According to Russian and U.S. intelligence sources, bin Laden, along with members of Al Qaeda's Shura Council, met with Chechen Mafia figures (including former KGB agents) in Grozny, Chechnya, where they made the deal to purchase 20 nuclear suitcases. For these weapons, bin Laden paid $30 million in a combination of cash and two types of heroin that had been refined in his laboratories. The street value of the heroin was in excess of $700 million.

After the devices were obtained, they were placed in the hands of Arab nuclear scientists who, federal sources say, "were probably trained at American universities."

As designed, the nuclear suitcases could only be operated by SPETNAZ (Soviet Special Forces) personnel. For that reason, Al Qaeda recruited former SPETNAZ troops to work on the project as technicians and trainers.

To overcome the technical problems of coded transmissions for the activation of the suitcase bombs, the Al Qaeda scientists came up with a way of hot-wiring the bombs to the bodies of soldiers seeking immediate martyrdom.

Nuclear suitcases are tactical rather than strategic weapons. They are not really suitcases, but suitcase-size nuclear devices. These weapons can be fired from grenade- or rocket-launchers or detonated by timing devices in public buildings, shopping malls, or sports arenas. One bomb placed in the center of a major metropolitan area is capable of instantly killing several hundred thousand civilians, while exposing millions of others to lethal gamma rays.

How real is the threat of nuclear suitcases?

Very real.

"There is no longer much doubt that bin Laden has finally succeeded in his quest for nuclear suicide bombs," says Yossef Bodansky, who headed the Congressional Task Force on Nonconventional Terrorism in Washington, D.C.

Bodansky's statement is supported by the testimony provided by former Russian security chief Alexander Lebed to the U.S. House of Representatives. Lebed said that 40 nuclear suitcases disappeared from the Russian arsenal after the collapse of the Soviet Union.

Bin Laden himself, in a December 1998 interview with *Time* magazine, suggested in an oblique way that he had secured nuclear weapons. When asked if he was seeking to obtain chemical or nuclear weapons, he answered "Acquiring weapons for the defense of Muslims is a religious duty. If I have indeed acquired these weapons, then I thank God for enabling me to do so."

When asked the same question by ABC News several weeks later, bin Laden responded in a similar manner, saying "If I seek to acquire such weapons, this is a religious duty. How we use them is up to us."

Former Secretary of Defense William S. Cohen stated in an addendum to the Pentagon report, "Proliferation: Threat and Response, 1997," that small amounts of weapons-usable plutonium and highly enriched uranium had been "diverted" from Russian nuclear facilities and could fall into the hands of terrorists. After the catastrophe of September 11, 2001, a federal official said "The question isn't whether bin Laden has nuclear weapons, it's when he will try to use them."

The flow of heroin from Afghanistan to Europe and the United States financed Al Qaeda's nuclear buys. Money from the Sicilian Mafia paid for the purchase of Chechnyan nuclear weapons from the Russian Mafia. The thread of Al Qaeda's jihad reached a whole new level, thanks to organized crime.

Chemical and Biological Weapons

But nuclear suitcases are not the only weapons of mass destruction at the disposal of Al Qaeda. The terrorist organization obtained chemical weapons from North Korea and Iraq.

Russian scientists recently confirmed that the former Soviet Union had produced large volumes of weapons-grade anthrax spores. The weapons were shipped to facilities in North Korea and Chechnya. Samples of the spores were sold by former KGB agents to Iraq. From Iraq the anthrax was delivered to Al Qaeda. The FBI confirms the information of sources who say that the anthrax spores were a gift to bin Laden from Saddam Hussein.

Anthrax is not the only biological weapon in the hands of Al Qaeda. The terrorist organization also has managed to obtain ...

- Plague viruses, including ebola and salmonella, from the former Soviet Union and Iraq.
- Samples of botulism biotoxin from the Czech Republic.
- Sarin from Iraq and North Korea.

Bin Laden realized how easy it would be to use these biological weapons against the United States. It would not require the hijacking of commercial jetliners but merely the use of a single-engine plane, a crop duster or a Piper Cub, so that a terrorist could sprinkle a small bag of white powder—powder composed of bacteriological spores—over a major metropolitan area.

The spores would infect tens of thousands, causing outbreaks of anthrax, smallpox, or pneumonic plague. Every contaminated infidel would infect thousands more—in grocery stores, shopping malls, theaters, sports stadiums, workplaces, schools, and churches. And these infected Americans would infect hundreds of thousands more ....

The mighty United States of America would be brought down not by a megaton bomb but by a simple microbe.

"The events in New York and Washington were tragedies beyond what anyone had previously imagined, but the potential of biological terrorism is far greater in terms of loss of life and destruction," Michael Osterholm, director of the University of the Minnesota's Center for Infectious Disease Research and Policy, told *The Washington Post* (September 17, 2001). "It would be less graphic—no flames and explosions—but much more insidious. Anyone with a cough would be a weapon."

The use of such weapons, bin Laden has indicated, would be fitting. During the Crusades, the Franks catapulted the rotting carcasses of horses and dogs and the bodies of plague victims over the walls of Antioch to spread death and disease among the Muslim people. The precedent had been set. Every action employed by the Christians in the past, bin Laden said, will elicit a similar reaction in the present.

The United States was not prepared for such warfare. In 1999 the U.S. General Accounting Office (GAO) discovered major gaps in the nation's system for protecting the populace against bioterrorism. The gaps included shortages of vaccines and medicines, stockpiles of expired drugs, and lax security measures where critical drugs were stored. The Centers for Disease Control and Prevention in Atlanta concluded in a 2001 report that America's public health system is "not adequate to detect and respond to a bioterrorist event." The anthrax letters sent to government officials and major media networks in 2001 (regardless of whether they prove to have been a domestic or an international act of terrorism) changed all that: Bioterrorism detection and response is now a national priority.

Bin Laden Weighs In

In a November 9, 2001, interview with Hamid Mir, a Pakistani journalist, Osama bin Laden justified his war against all Americans by saying ...

> "The American people should remember that they pay taxes to their government, they elect their president, their government manufactures arms and gives them to Israel, and Israel uses them to massacre Palestinians. The American Congress endorses all government measures and this proves that the entire America is responsible for the atrocities perpetrated against Muslims. The entire America because they elect the Congress."

Bin Laden told the interviewer that his war was against the American government, not the American people, but he added this:

> "We are carrying on the mission of our Prophet, Muhammad (peace be upon him). The mission is to

spread the word of God, not to indulge in massacring people. We ourselves are the targets of killings, destruction and atrocities. We are only defending ourselves. This is defensive jihad. We want to defend our people and our land. That is why I say that if we don't get security, the Americans, too, would not get security. This is a simple formula that even an American child can understand. This is the formula of live and let live."

Asked if he was attempting to acquire chemical and nuclear weapons, bin Laden said ...

"I heard the speech of American president Bush yesterday [October 9]. He was scaring the European countries that Osama wanted to attack with weapons of mass destruction. I wish to declare that if America used chemical or nuclear weapons against us, then we may retort with chemical and nuclear weapons. We have the weapons as deterrent."

Bin Laden, however, refused to tell the interviewer where the weapons came from. When pressed, he said "Go on to the next question."

Questioned about a political formula to end the war, bin Laden told Mir "You should ask this question to those who have started this war. We are only defending ourselves."

Bin Laden concluded ...

"Right now a great war of Islamic history is being fought in Afghanistan. All the big powers are united against Muslims. It is sawab to participate in this war."

Sawab is the Arabic term for "sacred duty."

12

Global Terrorism's
Many Fronts

"We are in uncharted waters. No one knows what
remains of the network outside Afghanistan .... We
don't know if there are cells that will emerge to try to
avenge bin Laden's elimination and whether there are
intermediate commanders in Europe or the United
States that remain operational."

—Olivier Roy, *The Financial Times,* November 30, 2001

On September 11, 2001, the attacks on the Pentagon and the
World Trade Center took the lives of more than 3,000 people. By
the end of the year, the United States–led coalition brought an
end to the Taliban's despotic rule of Afghanistan, destroyed Al
Qaeda's training camps and arsenals, killed a significant number
of Al Qaeda members in the intense bombing attacks of their
command centers, and have many others in detention.

As this book was going to press, the United States was on
high alert yet again for unspecified terrorist attacks that presumably had been in the planning stage for some time.

It is too early to assess the degree to which Al Qaeda's terrorism capabilities were diminished by the destruction of its
base. It also would be reckless to make too many assumptions

about the progress in the war on terrorism until more is understood about the potential of the global consortium of militant groups under the Al Qaeda umbrella.

What *is* known comes from a study called "Terrorism 2000," conducted in the year before the September 11 attacks. The study was prepared by Peter Probst of the Office of Defense Special Operations and Low-Intensity Conflict, along with an international team of experts on terrorism that included Major General Oleg Kalugin, former KGB head; a senior officer from Israel's Mossad; Brian Jenkins from the international security company, Kroll Associates; and Paul Wilkenson, professor of international relations at St. Andrew's University in Scotland, reputedly the best analyst of terrorist tactics in Europe.

The secret report was presented to representatives of the CIA, the FBI, the National Security Administration, the State Department, and the Defense Intelligence Agency. Like most government reports, it failed to spark a great deal of interest. Yet now, the report, which the State Department released to the public on April 30, 2001, seems not only incredibly relevant but also remarkably prophetic. It states the following:

- Weapons of mass destruction, thanks to the Russian Mafia, are now in the hands of Islamic terrorist groups who are plotting attacks on the United States.
- The Islamic terrorists, rather than bombing a single target, seem intent upon conducting simultaneous bombings and acts of carnage, creating a sense of the theatrical in their undertakings.
- The terrorists will engage in mass killing with chemical, biological, and radiological weapons.
- Terrorist groups will be less structured and hierarchical than they were in the past. Members of the same group

with the same objective may never meet before the time of their mission.

■ The terrorists will communicate by means of the Internet and cellular telephones, making it impossible to isolate their whereabouts, let alone to infiltrate their base of operations.

■ Religious zealotry will give rise to concurrent waves of mass-casualty operations.

"What is bad about all terror is when it is attached to religious and political abstractions and reductive myths that keep veering away from history and sense. This is where the secular consciousness has to try to make itself felt, whether in the United States or in the Middle East."

—Edward Said, *The Observer,* September 16, 2001

Simon Reeve, in his book, *The New Jackals* (Northeastern University Press, 1999), relates the following: "Some of the people thought the report was right on, but most of them thought it was too far out," said Marvin Cetron, president of Forecasting International, a firm that conducts studies for hundreds of major corporations and 17 governments from its base in Arlington, Virginia. "Some of the people said, 'My God, how can you believe that! They can't get hold of such things! Where are they going to get chemical or biological weapons?' They thought it was too far-fetched, and that people wouldn't go that far."

Now government officials are turning to the report with grave seriousness and raising questions that are no longer rhetorical: How can we stop the terrorist attacks? How can we neutralize a group like Al Qaeda? How did it all start? How will it all end?

The most unsettling question of all is: When will we know we've won? We know we won the battle against the Taliban because we knew who they were, where they were, and when they weren't in charge anymore. The war on terrorism is a war on an unknown number of people who live in an uncertain number of countries and have some potential—type and degree uncertain—to do us harm. So the answer is even more unsettling than the question: We won't know we've won until some period of time (unknown) elapses without a terrorist attack on Americans at home or abroad. The payoff on massive investments in intelligence-gathering, security, counterintelligence, freezing of assets, military preparedness, and so on will be fewer attacks and threats of attack.

Recently asked how U.S. military actions might affect Al Qaeda, J. T. Caruso of the FBI responded:

"It is too early to tell, from a law enforcement perspective, how the current military campaign in Afghanistan will affect Al Qaeda and its ability to operate in the future. Determination and vigilance will remain the keys to any success. It is one thing to disrupt an organization such as Al Qaeda; it is another to totally dismantle and destroy it. This must truly remain an international effort, with international cooperation on all levels, in order to be successful. All agencies within the U.S. government must remain vigilant and must continue to cooperate and work together in order to truly eradicate this scourge to all mankind everywhere known as Al Qaeda."

—J. T. Caruso, acting assistant director, Counter Terrorism Division, FBI (Congressional Statement, December 18, 2001)

Will military might do the job? There are historical examples of its effectiveness in destroying other Islamic militant groups; the infamous Assassins sect of Shi'a terrorists was wiped out by the Mongols in the thirteenth century. In the late nineteenth century, Muhammad Ahmad (the Mahdi) led a revolt against Egyptian rule in Sudan. It was put down by the British Army, and the group was never heard from again.

But these were homogeneous, local groups, not part of a far-flung global brotherhood united by their dedication to Al Qaeda's jihad.

Nicholas Lehmann, writing in *The New Yorker* (October 29, 2001), said that the United States will have to purchase the favor of Muslim countries by heaping helpings of foreign aid. He adds: "It would have to be a slow, careful, patient process that combines punishment of specific violent people with the offer of rewards for potential allies of the West."

Fouad Ajami, director of Mideast Studies at Johns Hopkins University, said on PBS's *Charlie Rose* (September 17, 2001) that "The Arabs' 'dowry' will be the United States position toward Israel," but that the United States should not respond to their pressure because their demands will not stop there. In another appearance on *Charlie Rose* (December 13, 2001) he said that if Osama bin Laden and Al Qaeda's leaders are destroyed, they'll be thought of as losers by their former admirers. "Win the war and everything will follow."

But others can see no way to end the attacks, arguing that terrorists such as bin Laden and al-Zawahiri do not seek rapprochement with the Western world but rather total annihilation of all that the Western world represents.

Oliver "Buck" Revell, the former deputy director of the FBI, said in a statement to the Committee on International

Relations of the U.S. House of Representatives (October 3, 2001): "Carlos the Jackal and Abu Nidal were essentially fighting for a place at the table. They wanted recognition for their movement, they wanted recognition for their demands, whereas Osama bin Laden and Ramzi Yousef want to punish and destroy. They're not looking for a place at the table. They want to destroy the table and maximize casualties." Revell refuses to believe that the death of bin Laden will have any impact on the proliferation of international terrorism, save the effect of fanning the flames.

The State Department is looking at long-term approaches, such as sponsoring counterterrorism initiatives in countries that are threatened by terrorist groups. It has already granted aid packages to some countries that have expressed their commitment to the war on terrorism, such as the Philippines, Turkey, and Uzbekistan. There is also a long list of uncommitted states that the offer of a counterterrorism partnership could, at a minimum, goad into demonstrating whether they are "with us or with the terrorists."

Fawaz A. Gerges, professor of Middle East and international affairs at Sarah Lawrence College, in a discussion on *Charlie Rose* (November 16, 2001) also takes a longer view. He pointed out that, although Osama bin Laden has done great damage to Islam by selectively choosing Islamic religious beliefs and traditions to support his terrorist agenda, his message does resonate in Muslim popular culture. Gerges thinks that the governments of countries such as Egypt and Saudi Arabia helped to create Al Qaeda by repressing dissident Islamic groups and punishing their members. The result was an escalation of violence by the militants followed by an escalation of repression by the governments, and on and on. He envisions a long-term role for the United States that would include showing less tolerance toward governments that prohibit free speech and lending more support to their efforts to nurture democratic principles.

"[Samuel P. Huntington, author of *The Clash of Civilizations and the Remaking of World Order*] observes that Osama bin Laden, for his part, clearly hopes to incite civilizational conflict between Islam and the West. The United States must prevent this from happening, chiefly by assembling a coalition against terrorism that crosses civilizational lines. Beyond that, the United States must take this opportunity to accomplish two things: first, to draw the nations of the West more tightly together; and second, to try to understand more realistically how the world looks through the eyes of other people. This is a time for a kind of tough-minded humility in our objectives and for an implacable but measured approach in our methods."

—Robert D. Kaplan, *The Atlantic Monthly,* December 2001

When did it begin?

Some say it began 1,300 years ago when the Prophet Muhammad received the teachings of the Koran.

Some say it began with the launching of the First Crusade by Pope Urban II in 1095.

Some say it began with the end of the Ottoman Empire in 1918.

Some say, with the centuries of British and French imperialism in the Middle East.

Some say, with the discovery of oil in Saudi Arabia and the creation of the Arabian American Oil Company in 1934.

Some say, with Israel's Declaration of Independence in 1948.

Some say, with the Iraqi invasion of Kuwait that gave rise to the Persian Gulf War, followed by an embargo that proved to be devastating for the Muslim people of Iraq.

Some say, with the emergence of repressive and secularized Muslim states in the Middle East and North Africa that encouraged militancy by excluding dissent from the national dialog.

How will it all end?

Most scholars agree that it will not end with the assassination of bin Laden or any of his Al Qaeda successors, or with the overthrow of Saddam Hussein and other extremist leaders in the Middle East.

Some diplomats think that Al Qaeda's role as an umbrella organization providing global reach will not be easily supplanted or duplicated, but many if not most of the splinters will wither. They observe that the terrorist training infrastructure previously offered by the chaotic state of Afghanistan could only be duplicated in scope elsewhere with great difficulty—and in the face of concerted international efforts to prevent it. Terrorism will not stop, in their view, but the momentum built up by Al Qaeda over the last 15 years or so will have been arrested and probably reversed.

Abou Khaled El Fadl, professor of Islamic Studies at the University of California, Los Angeles, said on *NBC News Dateline* (December 7, 2001) "I hope extremists will be marginalized, but Islamic tradition is vulnerable to hijacking groups. I don't have much hope that things are going to change in my lifetime."

But bin Laden thinks he knows how it will end. He wrote of the ending in a book called *America and the Third World War* that is circulated among his followers. It will end with the destruction of the Great Satan. It will end with the triumph of

Islam. It will end with the annihilation of Israel and the United States of America and a return to a Muslim polity that is ruled in the purist Islamic tradition.

"We predict," he writes in flowery Arabic, "a black day for America and the end of the United States as the United States. America will retreat from our land and collect the bodies of its sons from the battlefields. Allah willing."

> "Success or failure depends not on bin Laden; success or failure depends upon routing out terrorism where it may exist all around the world. He's just one person, a part of a network. And we're slowly, but surely, with determined fashion, routing that network out and bringing it to justice."

—President George W. Bush, October 11, 2001

A

Glossary

Ahl al Kitab "People of the Book," the phrase used by Muslims to designate Jews and Christians.

Al Aqsa Mosque in Jerusalem that is Islam's third holiest place.

Al Qaeda Arabic for "the Base," the umbrella organization founded in 1988 by Osama bin Laden, Muhammed Atef, and Ayman al-Zawahiri to carry on the jihad.

aliyah Literally "going up" in Hebrew, it is the word used for a wave of Jewish migration to Palestine, several of which occurred in the late nineteenth and early twentieth centuries.

Allahu akbar "God is greatest."

apostate One who has abandoned the faith.

ayah A verse of the Koran.

Ayatullah A senior Shi'a man of religion who has the authority to make religious rulings.

baksheesh Tip, bribe.

basmalah Introduction to each surah of the Koran and each Muslim prayer: "In the name of God, the Merciful, the Compassionate."

bayat Vow of allegiance.

burqa A garment that covers a woman from head to toe, so that no part of her body is visible.

caliph   One of a line of successors to the Prophet Muhammad. A caliph ruled as the adjudicator and enforcer of Islamic justice and guardian of the Muslim community.

caliphate   The institution ruled by a caliph. The last caliphate ended in 1918 with the end of the Ottoman Empire.

dhimmis   Jews and Christians (People of the Book) who submit to Muslim rule.

emir   Commander, or chief, in Muslim countries.

fatwa   An edict that was traditionally issued by religious or scholarly authorities but has come into use by Al Qaeda and other Islamic extremist groups.

fedayeen   Palestinian suicide squads of the mid-twentieth century.

Five Pillars   Rituals and practices of Islam in daily life: confession of faith (*Shahadah*), daily prayers (*Salat*), annual charitable donation (*Zakat*), fasting for the month of Ramadan (*Saum*), and the pilgrimage to Mecca (*Hajj*).

hadith   The body of sayings and acts attributed to the Prophet Muhammad.

hajj   A pilgrimage to Mecca. One of the Five Pillars of Islam.

harbis   Nonbelievers who refuse to submit to Islam.

hawalas   Traditional Middle Eastern system of transferring funds internationally without documentation.

Hazarahs   Ethnic group in Afghanistan that was part of the anti-Taliban coalition called the Northern Alliance.

Hijra   The Prophet Muhammad's flight from Mecca to Medina on July 16, 622, the first date of the Muslim calendar.

houris   Virgins.

imam   Guide, leader of the community.

jihad   Struggling, striving, holy war.

jinn Invisible spirits, some good and some evil. One of the seven basic beliefs of Islam.

kafir Infidel.

madrasah Religious school.

muazzin The one who calls the Ummah (Muslim community) to prayer.

Mujahedeen Warriors in a jihad; those who fought against the Soviet invasion of Afghanistan.

mullah A title of respect for someone who is learned in religious law.

qiblah The direction of Mecca, toward which Muslims pray.

Quraish Tribe to which the Prophet Muhammad belonged.

riddah Apostasy.

Salat *See* Five Pillars.

Saum *See* Five Pillars.

Shahadah *See* Five Pillars.

Shari'ah The body of laws that regulates Muslim life.

sheikh Chief.

Shi'a, Shi'as "Partisans of Ali"; a sect that grew from a group that originally supported Ali, the Prophet's son-in-law, as the first caliph to follow the Prophet. Shi'as represent approximately 15 percent of the world's Muslims and are mostly in Iran.

shirk Blasphemy.

shirks Faithless ones.

Shura Council Leadership council of Al Qaeda.

Sunnah The manner of conducting daily life.

Sunni The main body of Muslims, who follow the path (sunnah) of the Prophet Muhammad and the Koran and hadith (words and actions of the Prophet).

surah   A passage from the Koran.

Taliban   Literally, "students," who became the extreme fundamentalist militia of Pashtun Afghans and Pakistanis that overthrew the Afghan ethnic coalition government of Ahmad Shah Masood in 1998, and harbored Al Qaeda's leaders and training camps.

ulema   The body of scholars knowledgeable in Islam.

Ummah   The Muslim community.

Zakat   Required annual donation to charity. *See also* Five Pillars.

B

Bibliography

To come to grips with how life has changed since September 11, 2001, and what changes may lie ahead, it is not enough to increase our knowledge about Osama bin Laden and Al Qaeda. Global, supranational terrorism is now an integral part of our reality. To gain some understanding of what shape the future may take, we first have to go back—not just to the first attack on the World Trade Center in 1993—but all the way back—to the Judeo-Christian world, the birth of Islam, the Crusades, and the great empires.

I brought to this text my knowledge of history and the world's religions, as well as the access I've had through my work with the FBI to some of the people who sold the weapons, moved the heroin, and planted the bombs that have taken many innocent lives. I also gathered information from sources in government agencies and from official documents and trial transcripts.

To provide as broad a perspective as possible on the genesis of Al Qaeda, the militant Islamic groups in its sphere, and where the war on terrorism may lead, I drew on scholarly works, reportage, and opinion, for which I give attribution in the text. The following citations, listed by category, are given for books I relied on for insight, and those that are quoted or referred to in the text.

The Koran and the Prophet's Sayings

The transliterations of Arabic terms in the news follow Reuters style.

For translations of the Koran, I have relied on ...

Dawood N. J., trans. *The Koran.* New York: Penguin Books, 1974.

Malik, Muhammad F. A., trans. *The Holy Qur'an.* Houston: Islamic Society of Greater Houston, 1999.

Rodwell, J. M., trans. *The Koran.* London: Everyman, 1994.

For collections of the Prophet's sayings, I turned to the very readable translation ...

Arshed, Aneela Khalid'. *The Bounty of Allah.* New York: Crossroad Publishing, 1999.

An equally fine translation is ...

Khan, Maulana Wahiduddin. *An Islamic Treasury of Virtues.* New Delphi: Goodword Books, 1999.

The Life of Muhammad

For the life of the Prophet, my primary sources are ...

Al-Surhrawardy's, Allama Sir. *The Sayings of the Prophet.* Secaucus, NJ: Citadel, 1999.

Guillaume, A., ed. and trans. *The Life of Muhammad: A Translation of Ishaq's Sirat Rasul Allah.* London: Harper and Row, 1955.

Lings, Martin. *Muhammad: His Life Based on the Earliest Sources.* Rochester: Inner Traditions International, 1983.

I found the most useful secondary sources to be ...

Armstrong, Karen. *Muhammad: A Biography of the Prophet.* San Francisco: Harper San Francisco, 1993.

Cook, Michael. *Muhammad.* Oxford: Oxford University Press, 1983.

Peters, F. E. *Muhammad and the Origins of Islam.* Westminster: John Knox Press, 1993.

The Crusades

For the Crusades, there is my own book ...

Williams, Paul L. *The Complete Idiot's Guide to the Crusades.* Indianapolis: Alpha Books, 2001.

Which pales in comparison to the following:

Two books by the esteemed British scholar:

Billings, Malcolm. *The Cross and the Crescent.* New York: Sterling Publishing, 1990.

———. *The Crusades: Five Centuries of Holy Wars.* New York: Sterling Publishing, 1996.

And Robert Payne's great work:

Payne, Robert. *The Dream and the Tomb.* New York: Cooper Square Press, 1999.

Arab and Middle East History

I drew on these books for their overviews of the Middle East–North Africa region, Muslim Arabs, and the Israeli-Palestinian conflict.

Ajami, Fouad. *The Arab Perspective.* Cambridge: Cambridge University Press, 1981.

Bard, Mitchell. *The Complete Idiot's Guide to Middle East Conflict.* Indianapolis: Alpha Books, 1999.

Carmichael, Joel. *Arabs Today.* New York: Anchor Books, 1977.

Fromkin, David. *A Peace to End All Peace.* New York: Avon Books, 1989.

Hourani, Albert. *A History of the Arab People.* New York: Warner Books, 1992.

Lewis, Bernard. *The Middle East: 2,000 Years of History from the Rise of Christianity to Present Day.* New York: Touchstone, 1995.

Islamic History

Ahmed, Akbar. *Islam Today: A Short Introduction to the Muslim World.* London: I. B. Tauris, 1999.

Armstrong, Karen. *Islam: A Short History.* New York: The Modern Library, 2001.

Cragg, Kenneth, and R. Marsdon Speight. *Islam from Within: Anthology of a Religion.* Belmont, CA: Wadsworth, 1980.

Esposito, John. *The Oxford History of Islam.* Oxford: Oxford University Press, 2000.

Farah, Caesar E., Ph.D. *Islam, Fifth Edition.* New York: Barron's, 1994.

Hodgson, Marshall. *The Venture of Islam: Conscience and History in World Civilization.* Chicago: The University of Chicago Press, 1994.

Lapidus, Ira M. *A History of Islamic Societies.* Cambridge: Cambridge University Press, 1990.

Weiss, Walter M. *Islam.* New York: Barron's, 2000.

Islamic Fundamentalism

Appleby, R. Scott. *Spokesmen for the Despised: Fundamentalist Leaders of the Middle East.* Chicago: The University of Chicago Press, 1997.

Armstrong, Karen. *The Battle for God: Fundamentalism in Judaism, Christianity and Islam.* New York: HarperCollins, 2000.

Euben, Roxanne. *Enemy in the Mirror: Islamic Fundamentalism and the Limits of Modern Rationalism.* Princeton, NJ: Princeton University Press, 1999.

Mohadessin, Mohammad. *Islamic Fundamentalism: The New Global Threat.* New York: Seven Locks Press, 1993.

Qutb, Sayyed. *Signposts on the Path.* Cairo, 1964.

Jihad

Must reading for everyone on this subject ...

Ferogsi, Paul. *Jihad in the West: Muslim Conquests from the 7th to the 21st Centuries.* New York: Prometheus Books, 1998.

Firestone, Reuben. *Jihad: The Origin of the Holy War in Islam.* Oxford: Oxford University Press, 1999.

Johnson, James Turner. *The Holy War Idea in Western and Islamic Thought.* State College, PA: The Pennsylvania State University Press, 1997.

Lewis, Bernard. *The Political Language of Islam.* Chicago: The University of Chicago Press, 1988.

Wright, Robin. *Sacred Rage: The Wrath of Militant Islam.* New York: Simon & Schuster, 2001.

Terrorism

Barnaby, Frank. *Instruments of Terror: Mass Destruction Has Never Been So Easy.* London: Vision, 1997.

Beck, Aaron T. *Prisoners of Hate.* New York: Harper Trade, 2000.

Bowman, Stephen. *When the Eagle Screams: America's Vulnerability to Terrorism.* New York: Birch Lane, 1994.

Butler, Richard. *The Greatest Threat.* New York: Public Affairs, 2000.

Combs, Cindy. *Terrorism in the Twenty-First Century.* London: Prentice Hall, 1996.

Long, David E. *The Anatomy of Terrorism.* New York: Free Press, 1990.

Osama bin Laden and Al Qaeda

Alexander, Yonah, and Michael S. Swetnam. *Usama bin Laden's al-Qaida: Profile of a Terrorist Network*. Ardsley, NY: Transnational Publishers, 2001.

Bergen, Peter L. *Holy War, Inc.: Inside the Secret World of Osama Bin Laden*. New York: Free Press, 2001.

Bodansky, Yossef. *Bin Laden: The Man Who Declared War on America*. New York: Random House, 2001.

Hoffman, Bruce. *Inside Terrorism*. New York: Columbia University Press, 1999.

One of my favorite books is …

Pelton, Robert Young. *The World's Most Dangerous Places*. New York: HarperCollins, 2000.

For Osama bin Laden and Al Qaeda, I have gleaned information from Simon Reeve's riveting book:

Reeve, Simon. *The New Jackals: Ramzi Yousef, Osama Bin Laden, and the Future of Terrorism*. Boston: Northeastern University Press, 1999.

C

Resources

Books

For further reading on the subject of Al Qaeda and other Islamic terrorist groups, I highly recommend that you pick up a copy of ...

Reeve, Simon. *The New Jackals: Ramzi Yousef, Osama Bin Laden, and the Future of Terrorism.* Boston: Northeastern University Press, 1999.

The book is truly prophetic and speaks of the plans for several major attacks on the United States by bin Laden and his followers. Reeve is a highly respected investigative journalist who served for years as a staff writer for *The London Times*. His book is riveting and establishes the connection between the Oklahoma bombing and Ramzi Yousef, a connection that has escaped the attention of major news outlets.

Equally informative is ...

Rashid, Ahmed. *Taliban: Militant Islam, Oil, and Fundamentalism in Central Asia.* New Haven: Yale University Press, 2001.

Rashid, who covered the war in Afghanistan for more than 20 years for the international press, knows more about this subject than the collective talking heads of CNN. Particularly enlightening is his discussion of the drug connection between the Sicilian and Russian mafias and the Taliban and Al Qaeda.

Bodansky, Yossef. *Bin Laden: The Man Who Declared War on America.* New York: Random House, 2001.

Bodansky is an expert on international terrorism and chief consultant for the CIA. His *Bin Laden* book appeared in bookstores a few days before the events of September 11, 2001. It provides nightmarish insight into future threats that face the United States from the Muslim world, most notably from Iraq. But it is a remarkable book that should be read by every American.

Websites

On the following websites you'll find valuable information on Al Qaeda and get up-to-the-minute news about developments in terrorist activities around the world.

www.acpss.org/
Al-Ahram Center for Political and Strategic Studies

www.al-ayyam.com/
Al-Ayyam

www.arabnews.com/
Arab News (Saudi Arabia)

www.beiruttimes.com/
Beirut Times

www.dailystar.com.lb/
The Daily Star (Lebanon)

www.egy.com/
The Egyptian Gazette

www.iap.org/
Islamic Association for Palestine

wings.buffalo.edu/sa/muslim/isl/isl.html
Islamic texts

star.arabia.com/
The Jordan Star

www.metimes.com/
Middle East Times (Egypt)

www.intournet.com.il/icej
International Christian Embassy

www.gpo.gov.il/
Israeli Government Press Office

www.un.org/
United Nations

www.cdiss.org/hometemp.htm
The Center for Defense and International Security Studies

www.defenselink.mil/
DefenseLink

www.idf.il/
Israel Defense Forces

www.janes.com/
Jane's Information Group

www.leav-army.mil/fmso/
U.S. Army Foreign Military Studies Office

www.csis-scrs.gc.ca/
Canadian Security Intelligence Service

www.odci.gov/cia
Central Intelligence Agency

www.ict.org.il/
International Policy Institute for Counter Terrorism

www.terrorism.com/
The Terrorism Research Center

www.state.gov/www/global/terrorism/index.html
The U.S. State Department Office of Counter Terrorism

wwww.ari.net/mei/
The Middle East Institute

www.state.gov/index.html
U.S. State Department

www.washingtoninstitute.org/
The Washington Institute for Near East Policy

www.fbi.gov/majcases/summary.htm
The Federal Bureau of Investigation

Index

Canadian Security Intelligence Service
website, 201
Caruso, J. T., 180
cells, terrorist, 8, 82
spread of, 109
Center for Defense and International
Security Studies website, 201
Central Intelligence Agency website,
201
Cetron, Marvin, 179
Chamchi, Bouabide, 120
chemical weapons, Al Qaeda, 173
chemistry, formulation of, 43
Christian Crusades, 52, 54-59
first crusade, 54-55
fourth crusade, 57-58
second crusade, 55-56
third crusade, 57
Christian Solidarity, 85
Christianity, Sudan, holocaust, 86
circumference of the earth, calculation
of, 43
*Clash of Civilizations and the
Remaking of World Order, The*, 183
Clinton, William, 72, 145
failures of, 103
Cohen, William S., 173
committees
Finance, 7
Islamic Study, 7
Military, 7
Comnena, Alexis, 53
Consultation Council. *See* Shura
Council
conventional weapons, Al Qaeda, 168
Cox, Caroline, 87
Crusades (Christian), 52, 54-59
first crusade, 54-55
fourth crusade, 57

second crusade, 55-56
third crusade, 57-58

D

Dahoumane, Abdelmajid, 120
Daily Star, The (Lebanon) website,
200
Darkazanli, Mamoun, 108
Darra, Pakistan, arms dealers, 168
Davidic Psalms, 33
"Declaration of War Against the
Americans Occupying the Land of
the Two Holy Mosques," 129
Deek, Khalil Sa'id, 120
DefenseLink website, 201
Deir Yassin, massacre at, 66
demographics, Al Qaeda, 10
Desert Storm, 71
dhimmis (non-Muslims living in
Muslim states), 85, 128
Diaspora of the Jews, 61
Doha, Haydar Abu, 110
drug trade, Taliban, 164-166
Dubai Islamic Bank, terrorist funding,
167

E–F

East African missions, 12-15
East Jerusalem, Israeli occupation of,
69
Egypt, Islamic jijad, 77, 79
Egyptian Gazette website, 200
Eidarous, Ibrahim, 115
El Bara Bin Malik Division of the
Army of Liberating the Islamic
Holy Lands, 12
extremism, Islam, 45-49

S

Y–Z